JOB EVALUATION
A Critical Review

JOB EVALUATION
A Critical Review

BRYAN LIVY MA(LOND)
The City University

London
GEORGE ALLEN & UNWIN LTD
RUSKIN HOUSE   MUSEUM STREET

Printed in Great Britain
in 11 point Times Roman type
by the Aldine Press, Letchworth

Acknowledgements

I should like to express my gratitude to a number of organisations and individuals who have contributed to the preparation of this book. I am indebted to International Computers Limited, Associated Industrial Consultants/Inbucon Limited and the Post Office for their kind permission to reproduce case material in the appendixes. Individuals who have given me the benefit of consultation are numerous. Particularly I should like to acknowledge the advice and comments given on various parts of the book by my colleagues Sid Kessler and Dr Allan Williams at The City University's Graduate Business Centre. Professor John Child of the University of Aston in Birmingham (formerly of the London Graduate School for Business Studies) gave inspiration and encouragement from the inception. Nickie Fonda of Brunel University deciphered and typed up the manuscript. My sincere thanks to all. Needless to say, all matters of analysis, interpretation, judgement, opinion, error or omission are entirely my responsibility.

B. L. L.

Preface

I have written this book for both the lay and professional reader. I hope that it will be useful to students of management (particularly personnel management) at diploma, undergraduate or postgraduate level, and equally to established practitioners of job evaluation. To encompass such a wide spectrum I have tried to balance the emphasis given to fundamentals, examples, and to more theoretical abstractions. Although a number of works already exist in the field of job evaluation, they tend to treat the subject as a discrete collection of techniques and applications unrelated to other affiliated aspects of the working environment. I have tried to relate job evaluation to a wider personnel perspective. I have also presented the major developments in an historical framework. I hope nothing has been lost in lucidity, logical development or interest by painting a broad canvas.

B. L. L.
Graduate Business Centre
The City University
London

Contents

Chapter 1

Introduction

Job evaluation is over one hundred years old. At least according to one source first attempts at job evaluation were made in 1871 by the United States Civil Service Commission (Patton, Littlefield and Self, 1964). This was an isolated instance, and it was not until much later, until after the turn of the century, that any real interest began to develop. With the advent of scientific management and the birth of work study, industrialists began to consider wider aspects of productivity and related problem of remuneration, particularly for manual workers. Americans such as Merrill Lott and Eugene Benge devised schemes for job evaluation in the 1920s, the principles of which are still with us. But it was the rise of American industrial unions in the 1930s, and later, decisions of the US National War Labor Board which gave the impetus necessary to launch job evaluation as a major management technique. It came to Europe at about that time, although the first incidence this side of the Atlantic is attributed to the Swiss shoe company of Bally in 1918 (Bloch, 1951). In Britain its application is essentially a contemporary phenomenon. It was one of the many American ideas imported after the war aimed at making more effective use of manpower and increasing organisational efficiency. Its impact is now considerable.

Job evaluation is about money and work. How much is a job worth? How much does an individual job holder feel he should be paid? What is the value of the work to the employer? How might this value be determined? How might an equitable system for remuneration be arrived at? These are the questions job evaluation seeks to answer. Job evaluation is not a singular concept, but rather, as the British Standards Institution (1969) has chosen to define it, 'a generic term covering methods of determining the relative worth of jobs'.

13

There are numerous well-established ways of determining and administering systems of payment. Job evaluation is concerned with providing hard data on which to come to conclusions about the rate for the job. The processes of analysis and evaluation show up the essential differences between jobs, so that either quantitatively or qualitatively, decisions can be made about their relative worth. As such, job evaluation may be complementary to other procedures. It may, for instance, form the basis for joint negotiation of wages for manual workers and of salaries for staff employees. Alternatively, it might stand as almost the sole arbiter of pay.

Reliance on job evaluation alone is unlikely to be adequate. The theme of this book is that a broader view of remuneration and its associated issues, motivation, performance, participation, company policy and personnel administration should be taken. As a collection of techniques leading towards the mutual goals of improving an individual's job satisfaction and satisfactoriness of performance, job evaluation, properly established and seen in a wider perspective, can make a positive contribution. It cannot provide all the answers, but is not just another gimmick. It does not offer a quick solution to a crisis situation, but does offer the twin prospects of system and stability if planned for and developed on the bases of consensus, co-operation and concord.

It ought to be said at the outset that universal agreement about its merits and efficacy is lacking. Where controversy exists it has usually been engendered by suspicion, mistrust, misapplication of appropriate techniques, or the application of misappropriate ones, and occasionally, ignorance. There have been instances where job evaluation has been rejected by both management and unions. More often, however, its adoption has brought considerable benefits. Currently, resistance seems to be waning. Certainly, the incidence of job evaluation techniques is now widespread throughout industry, government and the armed services.

There are a number of interrelated reasons for its extended usage. Organisations are becoming more scientific and systematic through the introduction of a variety of management strategies. Growth, amalgamations, take-overs, stiff international competition, and in many cases shortages of skilled manpower, all combine to cause a critical appraisal of the workforce and subsequent rationalisation. With on-going social, technological and economic change, the content of jobs is inexorably altering also. With the demise of older, traditional jobs, new ones emerge to take their place. The problem of pay is therefore not static but part of the dynamically changing kaleidoscope.

Jobs have become deskilled, traditional demarcations blurred, and work roles and new specialisms have proliferated with the march of progress. Pay scales have become intricate, especially on the shop floor. The National Board for Prices and Incomes survey (Report No. 83, 1968) found that in many companies 'job and rates had evolved separately and in such a way that any apparent relationship between the two things had been lost', and further that 'the distinct purposes for which the different components in individual pay existed had been obscured'. Irrationality between jobs and pay scales has often come about from pressures brought to bear at particular times in the past, so that in many firms a large or even unknown number of grades may exist, with different payment schemes or allowances hitherto introduced now serving to distort basic pay scales.

The problem is further exacerbated where traditional notions of skilled, semi-skilled and unskilled work still form the basis of remuneration. The anachronism is often perpetuated despite the fact that technological change has served to limit the degree of skill required and redistribute it across a wider range of jobs. The skill factor taken alone as a determinant of income is no longer justified, although one still finds that craftsmen tend to be paid for the skills they possess rather than exercise. Then there is the added proliferation of white-collar jobs. Staff specialisms are increasing as a function of more sophisticated management. Salaries are a rapidly increasing element of the total payroll budget, and the growth of white-collar unionism is giving impetus to job evaluation and related techniques.

With increasing specialisation and division of labour, larger numbers of people are employed in similar jobs, often in the same work-place, and are provided with comparisons of relative pay. Whatever standards of measurement are used, subjective or scientific, individuals invariably assess the fairness of payment received for a job in relation to the earnings of other workers. This is the crux of the pay determination problem —assessing and agreeing the fairness of differential pay. The problem confronts every manager, trade unionist and employee in business today. Sadly there is ample evidence in the form of industrial unrest,

15

attesting that the matter is being dealt with less than satisfactorily. Issues affecting earnings can become a major source of dissatisfaction and conflict between employer and employee when pay is not felt to reflect the true worth of a job, however that worth may be perceived by an individual or group.

Moreover, post-war Britain has experienced a situation of near full employment and rising standards of living. It has also seen a great deal of dehumanisation of work. Perhaps associated with affluence and alienation, there is evidence of a withdrawal from work as a central life interest (Goldthorpe *et al.*, 1968; Hulin and Blood, 1968). As a result, income may be assuming more than its role as a satisfier of basic needs, to become a measure of an individual's status and standing in the community at large and an instrument for optimising off-the-job leisure. For most people, pay is a matter of personal concern as well as one of the rewards of labour. In times of rapid inflation it assumes crucial importance.

The substance of this book is devoted to a consideration of the main techniques of job evaluation as a determinant of income. The approach is intended to be critical and yet constructive. Predominant concern is with operational aspects, but to an extent, also with behavioural consequences. The lay-out should be self-explanatory as per the chapter headings. The main methods and how they might be applied are explained and illustrated. We begin with a consideration of the relative importance of pay to an individual employee, and a review is made of the main psychological theories regarding the motivational power of money and its relative importance as a satisfaction to be derived from work. Attention is paid to the way in which job evaluation ought to be set up, and after an analysis of the various techniques, examples are given of some of the better known applications. Throughout, the book tends to concentrate on salaried staff rather more than manual workers, although not exclusively, for a relatively larger proportion of the salariat are covered by job evaluation methods. Finally, an overview is attempted of the wider issues affecting salary administration. A résumé of the main points appears in the concluding summary.

16

Chapter 2

Socio-Psychological Aspects of Pay

The purpose of this chapter is to make an attempt at explaining and unravelling some of the mysteries and uncertainties which surround the role which money, as a reward for work, plays as a motivator of human behaviour and performance. Over the last half-century or so views have changed as to its relative importance, but the fact which has remained consistent is that money is still a sensitive and crucial element of the reward-compensation package. Issues affecting payment for work, the rate for the job, the grade or scale of payment, questions of differentials, bonuses, incentives and the like are all capable of evoking very powerful emotions. One may notice, almost any week of the year, the number of strikes and other industrial disputes which are expressed largely in terms of pay, although it is true, other factors may be involved. One may notice the continual round of negotiations, the constant battle against inflation, professed concern for the less well paid, anxiety about job security, and endless discussion about a host of factors which might affect the stability of a regular, adequate income. There can be no doubt that in a market economy, work and payment are inseparable. Without money, people are unable to buy the goods and services necessary for survival; they cannot advance in status in the eyes of their fellow men; nor can they make material improvements in their standards of living. If the work is difficult, dangerous, boring, demanding, degrading, people expect appropriate compensation. For some, the satisfactions derived from work may in themselves be adequate, or form at least partial compensation. But for many this is not so, and it is not surprising to see a more instrumental attitude emerge.

The factors which influence people's levels of expectation concerning rewards, including payment, have been the subject of considerable research and theorising. Behavioural scientists have produced a number of models which seek to explain the relationship between pay and work, and which seek to provide some understanding of the role money plays as a motivating force. Because of the intricacies and complexities of a wide number of issues involved, the models which have been put forward reduce the problem, of necessity, to a number of key variables. The result is, therefore, that they have to be simplistic in their explanations of behaviour. They cannot always provide complete answers, nor do they have universal validity. The trouble is that the goals of a concise, acceptable model of behaviour, on the one hand, and on the other, of a complete appreciation of the complex interaction of drives, rewards, attitudes and responses of a creature so variable and complex as *homo sapiens*, are mutually exclusive. The corollary is that a theoretical model of convenient, manageable proportions, albeit based on empirical research evidence, cannot always be used as a predictor of behaviour in other situations. The problem is further confounded by the fact that the models which have been produced are often controversial, and indeed, sometimes conflicting. Generally speaking, the most simple models are the ones which have led to the most confusion; the ones which on the surface appear to present the tidiest explanation are the very ones which conceal the myriad pathways of the maze.

Most of the controversial debate centres around the relative importance of money *vis-à-vis* other factors such as job satisfaction, group norms, intrinsic rewards from work, levels of responsibility, influence and recognition. The emphasis which has been placed on money has varied historically, and there has tended in recent years for more consideration to be given to non-monetary factors. This shift has been partly due to the changing nature of industrial society, the growth of automated processes and their effects on job design, to changes in worker aspirations, collective organisation at work, and not least to the research findings of behavioural scientists working in industry. Unfortunately, some of the research evidence is open to criticism, either on grounds of methodology or upon doubts about conclusions which have been reached. This has not helped to clear the air. The polemic ranges from those who believe money to be the prime motivator to those who would accord it negative value as a motivator.

Traditionally, of course, money, profits, financial incentives, material acquisitions have been used as the carrots to increase production since the industrial revolution, and it is not surprising that a certain amount of conditioning of people's attitudes has taken place. It is only relatively recently that we have witnessed a growing awareness of the wider rewards which can and should derive from work. The idea of money as a prime motivator dies hard. The cultural forces in modern industrial society have roots in the past. The development of monopoly capitalism has been closely associated with changes in man's moral, social and religious values. The progenitor of modern capitalism was a medieval system, in which a man plied his craft, and in which to all intents and purposes, capital was the servant of the man. Man exercised a high degree of control over the means of production—his individual decisions were critical—and the cycle from raw material to finished product and end use were well within the limits of his comprehension. What, later, has been termed the 'Zeigarnik' effect—that is the ability to see and influence the complete operational cycle, and from which considerable job satisfaction is thought to derive—is well illustrated at this level of technology.

Technology subsequently developed faster than man's individual capacity to influence it or even to comprehend its full ramifications. Capital became the master. Man became isolated and estranged from his own invention. Man's labour became an instrument in the service of the great machine. In many respects man's mutation did not accelerate with the pace of capital growth, division of labour, functional specialisation, automation, rationalisation of production, and so on. As Herzberg (1968) has noted: 'Unfortunately, the knowledge man has obtained about the human condition continues to fall far behind his phenomenal progress in solving problems in his environment.' Not surprisingly signs of maladjustment became evident, most clearly manifest in the degree of instrumentality existing between employer and employee, and to some extent in manifestations of neurotic anxiety and insecurity. Man became a commodity to be bought and sold just like the commodities he produced. Karl Marx first drew attention to what he called the 'fetishism of commodities', and in order to produce them, an industrial system resulting in the 'alienation of labour', or in other words a feeling on the part of the worker of being separated from the means of production which he does not own and cannot control. Changes in commercial life were brought about not only by invention and discovery, but also by changes in religious values. 'Theological doctrines had created an acute sense of uncertainty concerning salvation which intensified the work habits and the asceticism of the parishioners, and consequently gave great impetus to the development of entrepreneurial activity. This Puritan credo became secularised as the concern with uncertainty decreased and as men became more confident in the foreordained coincidence between virtue and success' (Bendix, 1956). In other words, the religious ethic justified the cataclysmic changes in life-styles, crafts and patterns of work brought about by the industrial revolution. Commercial success became a virtue. Economic man was born.

The antecedents of a culture cannot be ignored. Industrialisation has had a conditioning influence, under which mankind has learned to accept certain values imposed upon him by the system. It was not until the work of an American, Frederick Winslow Taylor (1911), that some of these ideas became crystallised into a theory of industrial motivation —ideas which are now regarded as somewhat primitive. What Taylor epitomises is the Protestant ethic—the master-servant relationship in which both parties are predominantly economically motivated, competitive and self-interested. The reason why Taylor's success was limited, and the reason why the so-called 'principles of scientific management' do not work, on the whole, when applied to individual, group or team activities in modern organisations is that they are based on traditional, but ill-founded, assumptions about the nature of human needs and behaviour. The assumptions are that people only try to satisfy economic needs at work—the only reward they seek is money; that people's behaviour is always rational in the pursuit of that goal—they always try to maximise their rewards in return for an instrumental and calculated amount of effort; emotional needs do not enter the picture; and that the interests of the worker and employer are mutual—no conflict exists between the two. Furthermore the well-being of the individual (measured only in economic terms) is inextricably linked to the well-being of the firm (measured only in economic terms). No mobility of labour is assumed possible—hence a policy geared to deflation and unemployment, in which the threat of dismissal is the stick, offset by the carrot, a wage-packet pure and simple.

Douglas McGregor (1960) summed up the tenets of this philosophy in what he called Theory X: Management has sole responsibility for organising men, money, materials and machines in the pursuit of profit.

The activities, aspirations and attitudes of people working in the organisation must therefore be modified to fit in with the organisational goals. People are basically lazy, have an inherent dislike of work or responsibility, and must if necessary be coerced or punished. People are resistant to change, insecure (not surprisingly) and prefer to be led. All powers of direction and control are vested in management, who autocratically shall decide what is to be done, how it is to be done, and what is good for the employee.

In the light of modern theory, such views are anachronistic. There is little evidence to support the view that man is primarily money-motivated, that he is by nature competitive and interested only in his economic wellbeing. Taylor's work was in fact the first of a series of experiments and investigations into industrial behaviour. His insistence on money as a prime motivator refers at best to an *ex post facto* situation, to the assumptions which had guided management philosophy since the industrial revolution. Latterly those ideas have been refuted. It is now generally agreed that money by itself will not provide magic solutions to problems of motivation and productivity. This is not to imply that money is unimportant, far from it, but rather to pose the question of its relative importance to other motivators, and to pose the questions: What level of payment will be regarded as equitable and satisfactory? How did a change of emphasis come about? What evidence is there for taking a wider view?

An Australian, Elton Mayo, working as a management consultant in America, revealed some important considerations almost by accident. Together with a group of fellow researchers investigating industrial efficiency, Mayo conducted a series of experiments at the Hawthorne plant of the Western Electric Company, near Chicago, Illinois. The famous 'Hawthorne' experiments were an important landmark in the development of behavioural theory, if for no other reason than the fact that they looked beyond the individual working in isolation, and considered the total group and sub-group in interaction. Unfortunately, few experiments have generated more confusion and misunderstanding. The conclusions which have sometimes been drawn cannot always irrefutably be substantiated from the evidence. In a number of respects, controlled and rigorous experimental methodology is lacking. Of course, it is easy to criticise pioneer studies in hindsight, and it is only fair to add that the studies were not originally intended as paragons

21

of experimental virtue anyway, but were rather a series of reports of investigations in which a number of variables which could be construed to have an effect on work performance were changed. For example, a commonly asserted claim is that they stress the relative subordination of financial rewards in favour of social ones. The exact truth of the matter is sometimes difficult to discern. Having issued a caveat, let us examine some of the details.

About 30,000 workers at the plant were concerned with the manufacture of electrical goods. The experiments consisted of a few, small, specially selected samples of employees, most of whom were female. The activities investigated were confined to certain areas—mainly coil winding, relay assembly, mica splitting and bank wiring operations and some inspection jobs. Constraints imposed by technology and politics often mean that researches in organisations have to be confined in some way. The experiments were conducted in two phases. The first phase (1924–7) in conjunction with the National Research Council of America investigated the effects of changes in illumination on productivity, and showed without doubt that there were certain factors at work apart from physical ones (in this case lighting) which affected the motivation and productivity of a group of workers. The illumination studies were really the harbinger of the main body of research, and the earlier findings in many ways coloured and anticipated later findings. In the second phase (1927–32) Mayo co-operated with Roethlisberger and Dickson from the Harvard School of Business Administration, and the investigations consisted of four main experiments in relay assembly and mica-splitting test rooms and in the bank wiring observation room. These findings are much more equivocal.

The first study (in the second phase) in a relay assembly test room, involved five girls for an experimental period of two years. Changes were made in their working conditions, in their hours of work, in the length and periodicity of rest pauses, in the tasks which as individuals they had to perform, in the styles of supervision, and in the incentive payment scheme which was changed according to their preferences. At the end of the experiment, output had risen 30 per cent (Roethlisberger and Dickson, 1939), but as Alex Carey (1967) points out, it is impossible to identify any one variable as having had a significant causal effect on the outcome, since the changes were introduced cumulatively over time, and no control group was set up. Leadership style was very much influenced by output. For the first three and a half months it was relaxed and friendly, followed by seven months of a sterner more autocratic style during which period two girls were dismissed. They were replaced by two others, selected in the hope they would be more positively motivated. When output rose, supervision was relaxed again. Apart from the cardinal sins of a 40 per cent mortality rate in the experiment and no appropriate control data, it is not possible from this study to draw any firm conclusions as to the influence of supervision, the physical context of work or the motivating power of money.

The second study again involved five girls engaged in relay assembly work, who were selected from the normal working department of some one hundred girls. They were allowed, as in the first experiment, to select a wage incentive system based on their own average output, in accordance with policy in the department as a whole, where payment was similarly based on average output. The five girls in the experimental group worked harder and output rose 12·6 per cent (Roethlisberger and Dickson, 1939), and their earnings improved accordingly. Such was the consternation of the rest of the department, whose output had remained stable, that the preferred incentive scheme in the experimental group had to be disbanded—whereupon the output of the five girls dropped 16 per cent (Roethlisberger and Dickson, 1939). Professor Morris Viteles (1954) remarks that this 'represents evidence ordinarily interpreted as indicative of the direct and favourable influence of financial incentives upon output'. The results also allude to the group norms (i.e. standard, accepted patterns of behaviour) influencing output in the main department, and for which there is clearer evidence in the later bank wiring observation room study. The original high output of the experimental group may have been due to greater group cohesion (morale), better communications and relationships which obtain in smaller groups, or a higher degree of money motivation, or simply to what has been christened the 'Hawthorne effect', the implications of which are that any group or individual selected as an object of interest will acquire kudos or ego-satisfaction which may well have a positive effect on performance.

A third study was conducted with a further five girls in a mica splitting room, physically separated from the main assembly operations, with a view to replicating the changes in hours of work, rest pauses and friendly styles of supervision introduced in the first study, but away from the direct influence of the other girls. Although output is reported to have increased (due to which variables?) no viable comparisons are possible with the earlier studies, since the incentive scheme was changed and the girls were working on quite different tasks.

The bank wiring observation room study is perhaps of more significance. A working team of fourteen men engaged in wiring and soldering banks of equipment, together with two inspectors, were placed under observation. Two cohesive sub-groups developed, each with norms of production for a fair day's work. Considerable social pressure, in the form of various verbal censures or ostracism, was placed informally by the group on its members to conform to an accepted level of output. Social membership of a group can be seen most clearly here as a prime factor influencing productivity. It is worth noting that one group thought itself of higher status, and were consistently higher producers. However, financial considerations are not necessarily discredited. As A. J. M. Sykes (1965) has pointed out, the men thought that if production rose to too high a level, the rates would be cut, for the company had a reputation for restructuring rates and jobs. The production norms may not have arisen for social reasons, but as a deliberate attempt to deceive management.

Out of the confusion which surrounds the Hawthorne studies, a number of points emerge. They provide insufficient evidence to refute the money incentive. They do suggest that motivation and productivity are the result of complex behaviour patterns, and can be influenced by a range of variables. Time and motion studies and the physical conditions of work are clearly not the whole story. The studies, although controversial, induced a shift of emphasis away from physical factors on to the higher plane of people's mental attitudes to work. They added the rider to the previous simplistic views of industrial behaviour, that in order to motivate, one must know to what incentives people will be responsive. One must have some idea of the needs which people seek to satisfy, and so far as is possible, structure the working environment to provide opportunities for the satisfaction of these needs.

One of the revered conceptual models which focuses on the satisfaction of human needs is the one developed by Abraham Maslow (1943, 1954), arising out of the earlier work of Goldstein (1939). Maslow postulates that man is basically a 'wanting animal'. His life-style is predominatly directed towards satisfying his various wants. As each want becomes sated, new wants arise. From the moment of birth, an unending chain-reaction is set in motion. There is a general development from the seeking of satisfaction of primordial needs basic to the existence of life itself, through a series of levels, to the pursuit of satisfactions on higher intellectual, cultural and social planes. Maslow organised his categories of human needs into a hierarchy of importance:

1. *Physiological Needs* essential to biological survival, such as food and water, air to breathe, physical activity, sleep and rest, sex. When these needs are catered for, man then needs:

2. *Safety and Protection* in order to safeguard what has already been accomplished. This takes the form not only of somewhere to live, but also of a stable, non-hostile environment.

3. *Love Needs*, in the widest sense, then become apparent, i.e. friendly working relationships with other individuals, recognition by one's peers as a fellow group-member.

4. *Esteem Needs* then arise, in which the individual seeks a properly founded self-respect and the esteem of others, arising out of his own unique contribution to society, and leading to the highest level of:

5. *Self-Actualisation Needs*. One needs to develop one's skills, capacities and aptitudes to the full, to develop into a whole man (or woman).

Two ideas are inherent in this hierarchy. First, the idea of prepotency, in other words, that higher level needs do not become operative until the respective lower needs have been satisfied. This view is open to debate, in the light of differences which exist between individuals in terms of their need states and the opportunities which may be available for satisfying them, and moreover the fact that it is conceivably possible for more than one need to be operative simultaneously and for opportunities for higher need satisfaction to present themselves first. If this rider is accepted, then the concept is dubious, since there can be no criterion for ranking needs on hierarchical grounds. However, this is a moot point. Second, and perhaps more important, is the idea that a need which has already been satisfied cannot be a motivator, since it is not likely to incite new goal-directed behaviour. A need which has not been satisfied is more likely to stimulate and call forth new behaviour patterns. Money is not mentioned. Clearly, in a market economy, it is a useful, necessary, agent for satisfying the two lower-level needs.

25

The implication of Maslow's theory for practice are that an adequate income is a prerequisite for survival, but if the hierarchy is valid, money is not likely to motivate the satisfaction of self-actualisation needs. Instead, higher-level needs are more likely to be satisfied by the opportunity and freedom to develop one's potentialities. Some research by Porter (1961, 1962, 1963) has shown, in summary, that in industrial and commercial organisations, the opportunities for need satisfaction tend to be rather limited at junior staff and operative levels of work, that opportunities increase as one ascends into the higher echelons, and that self-actualisation needs are the ones least satisfied at all levels of an organisation.

It was this kind of thinking about human needs and motives, and the opportunities (or lack of them) for their expression in organisational life that led to the formulation of Douglas McGregor's Theory Y (1960). Theories X and Y were presented as polarisations of management ethos. The main tenets of Theory Y are that man has a natural capacity for creativity, imagination and intellectual development. He seeks scope to deploy his talents, and will expend considerable energy in the pursuit of goals to which he is committed. He needs to be motivated, therefore, on a higher level than simple carrot-and-stick philosophy. This is very much in the tradition of the 'human relations school' which blossomed after Hawthorne. Although we have acknowledged the existence of motivational factors other than money, we have not, until this point in the exposition, sought to clarify the *relative* importance which money has *vis-à-vis* these other factors.

The work which has become classic in this connection is that of Frederick Herzberg and his colleagues. Herzberg, Mausner and Snyderman (1959) published the results of an investigation into the origins of job satisfaction and job dissatisfaction of some 200 engineers and accountants employed in nine separate companies. The investigation was based on individual interviews in which respondents were asked to identify and relate what they felt to be the critical incidents in their jobs which had given rise to exceptionally good feelings and to exceptionally bad feelings. The idea was not just to collect a series of psychological reactions, but to pinpoint objective happenings. Some 5,000 statements were classified, and the data were broken down to specific events. Two distinct sets of variables and related attitudes emerged from the study. The things which appeared to be closely associated with high job satisfaction (what Herzberg calls the 'satisfiers') differed from those associated with low job satisfaction ('dissatisfiers'). Herzberg identified what appeared to be a natural dichotomy in the influences at work which gave rise to satisfaction and dissatisfaction. There appeared to be at least an associational relationship, and maybe a causal one, between the elements of work concerned with the content of the job proper (i.e. the work itself, responsibility, advancement, recognition and achievement) which contained the seeds of personal satisfaction for the incumbent, and on the other side of the coin, the elements of work concerned with the context or environment in which it operates (i.e. company policy, styles of supervision, salary levels, interpersonal relationships and working conditions) which could contain the seeds of personal dissatisfaction. Herzberg postulated that this dichotomy in the sources of personal happiness at work emanated directly from the duality of man's basic nature. On the one hand, man is an animal, and seeks to avoid pain and find pleasure in the things which relate to his environment. He is hedonistic. On the other hand, man is endowed with prolific natural capacities which make him unique as an animal, and he seeks opportunities for psychological growth, development or 'self-actualisation'. These concepts form the basis of Herzberg's 'two-factor' theory.

Aspects of work which relate to the job context or environment can result in dissatisfaction because of the need to avoid unpleasantness. It is vital, therefore, that they obtain at satisfactory levels for the individual, and have been variously labelled 'maintenance factors', 'hygiene factors' or 'dissatisfiers'. The important point is that although hygiene factors can be a potential source of dissatisfaction, for hedonistic reasons, because they do not provide *at work* outlets for man's aspirations for growth, they cannot be primary sources of job satisfaction.

The sources of satisfaction, or outlets for self-actualisation and the achievement of growth, derive from those factors which relate to the content of the job and work itself. They have been variously labelled 'motivators' or 'satisfiers'. Herzberg's two sets of factors are quite separate and distinct. They are both unipolar. The 'dissatisfiers' can cause dissatisfaction at one extreme but not satisfaction at the other, simply an acceptable level of maintenance. The 'satisfiers' can cause satisfaction, but at the other end of the scale, not dissatisfaction, simply 'no job satisfaction'. The questions which are of concern for our purposes, are first of all the validity of the theory, and secondly, can we be more specific about the relative importance of salary in all this? Both questions are difficult to answer.

The fundamentals of Herzberg's two-factor theory have been substantiated in a few studies (e.g. Schwarz, Jenusaitis and Stark (1963) and Myers (1964)), but have not been replicated elsewhere (e.g. Dunnette (1965) and Porter (1964)), and the whole methodology of Herzberg's research has engendered considerable criticism (House and Wigdor, 1967). One of the main criticisms is that the idea of two factors is a grossly oversimplified theory of motivation. It also ignores cognitive (i.e. intellectual) and conative or affective differences (i.e. feelings and emotions) as between individuals. The general impression is that even if one does not know all the answers, one at least knows that there is a good deal more to it than Herzberg postulates.

Hermann Hesse (1927) in his novel *Steppenwolf* probably got nearer the truth when he said: 'Man is an onion made up of a hundred integuments, a texture made up of many threads.' Further, the Herzberg study was open to all the subjective misconceptions which self-report surveys are liable to. One can question the desire of respondents to report accurately, even if they are aware objectively of the events which cause them satisfaction or frustration. It has been contended that there is a tendency to attribute things which go well to one's own achievement and to blame others for the things which go wrong, a simple ego-defensive mechanism. Moreover, can the findings of two particular occupational groups—engineers and accountants—be generalised upon? Is what may be true of professional workers, who have opportunities for increased responsibility and advancement, equally true of blue-collar operatives geared to the machine or assembly line? Do professionals find work itself more satisfying because it is inherently richer than screwing bolts or clerking invoices all day? Why do professionals seek responsibility and advancement—for the intrinsic rewards that it brings, or increased salary and status, or both? Put another way, there may well be co-variance between variables in the two sets of factors, disguised by semantics. To be specific, 'advancement' and 'recognition' could both be interpreted to contain connotations of remuneration.

Herzberg's theory also ignores the relationship between effort and performance, and effort and reward, and the implications of the expectancy

28

theory of motivation, the refinements of which chronologically succeeded Herzberg's work, and to which we shall turn our attention presently. Herzberg does acknowledge that affective behaviour can be influenced by personality characteristics. Some of his respondents did claim to derive job satisfaction purely from hygiene factors. Herzberg rather sweepingly divides people into 'motivation seekers' and 'maintenance seekers'; confining his analysis purely to work roles, ignoring interests and activities outside of work, and assuming that the latter group have not reached a very high degree of personal adjustment. He sees them only on a lower level seeking to satisfy avoidance needs. 'The neurotic motivation pattern of hygiene seeking is mostly a learned process that arises from the value systems endemic in society' (Herzberg, 1968). Maybe, maybe not. The fact is that, rightly or wrongly, the phenomenon exists and is not uncommon. In a study of a sample of managers made by Porter (1961), some 80 per cent expressed dissatisfaction with their pay and sought higher pay as one of their primary goals. Depending upon how you look at it, pay *can* be seen as a reward or recognition for effort and performance and so contribute to personal satisfaction.

Herzberg's thesis, although not explicit, is concerned with moral and political issues, and is in that sense re-educative, rather than attempting to satisfy *status quo* values about motivation and reward. Hence his pursuit of 'job enrichment' as an agent for harnessing the aspirations of people at work. Meanwhile, we live in a monetary exchange society, and Herzberg does not tell us very clearly how to take the steps to a more utopian society from a rather barren pursuit of money without causing dislocation. It is all a question of balance.

The two-factor theory hinges partly on the link between a factor and its durability or potency as a source of satisfaction or dissatisfaction over time. Herzberg distinguishes between long-term and short-term effects. Of the 'satisfiers', work itself, responsibility and advancement were found to have the most lasting value and to make for the most positive attitudes to work. For this reason, coupled with the high frequency of their occurrence in the anecdotal reporting of respondents, they are regarded as the most significant motivators. As far as monetary rewards are concerned, their powers of satisfaction are short-lived, and in the long run become impotent. Monetary rewards lead to the avoidance of economic deprivation, but are seen as no more than 'briefly

29

acting analgesics for meaningless work', and indeed, 'as an affector of job attitudes, salary has more potency as a job dissatisfier than as a job satisfier' (Herzberg, 1968). Two points need to be made. In the first place, even if the contention were correct, it is clearly of fundamental importance to get the money right, to get the money part of the work contract at a fair and acceptable level, for no motivation at all is going to take place in the absence of hygiene factors. One might argue that the hygiene factors are the foundations on which to build opportunities for the satisfaction of higher level needs. In the second place, the basic premise from which Herzberg makes his deductions is not strictly upheld by the statistical evidence. As Opsahl and Dunnette (1966) succinctly put it:

'In all of the descriptions of unusually good job feelings, salary was mentioned as a major reason for the feelings 19 per cent of the time. Of the unusually good job feelings that lasted several months, salary was reported as a causal factor 22 per cent of the time; of the short-term feelings, it was a factor 5 per cent of the time. In contrast, salary was named as a major cause of unusually bad job feelings only 13 per cent of the time. Of the unusually bad job feelings lasting several months, it was mentioned only 18 per cent of the time (in contrast with the 22 per cent of long-term good feelings mentioned above). . . . These data seem inconsistent with the interpretations and lend no substantial support to hypotheses of a so-called differential role for money in leading to job satisfaction or job dissatisfaction.'

The key to the secrets of motivation is elusive, and perhaps we should look a little deeper into the basic drives and responses of human organisms. Psychologists working in experimental and clinical fields have again produced a plethora of theories, and from what may at times appear a confusing picture, it might be desirable to draw out the main threads of the principal psychological ideas. We have drawn attention already to the existence of need states in human organisms. Were it not for these need states, we as humans would be largely inactive in a strictly motivational sense. The reflex actions to which we are liable are not really 'motivated' in the strict sense of the word. Motivation can be regarded as the process of satisfying a particular need, that need itself being caused by a state of deprivation. The need to satisfy or consummate such a state of deprivation gives rise to drives which are directed towards a goal-object, perceived by the individuals as being capable of producing or bestowing the desired satisfaction. Motivation, then, has two aspects to it: the activation and the direction which it takes. The directional aspect is also two-edged: there is the positive aspect of moving towards a particular goal, and the negative aspect of moving away from an undesired state, for example the aversive physiological drives which lead us away from pain. These ideas form the basis of the so-called 'need-path-goal' hypothesis, a development of Kurt Lewin's (1935, 1936) 'field theory', in which an individual finds himself in his 'life-space', a conceptual field similar to a force-field in physics, and in which he is subject to various pressures, internal and external obstacles, and the plurality of possible courses of action. Lewin emphasises the unity and wholeness of man's psychology in the same way that Gestalt psychology does. In a sense it is perhaps wrong to distinguish man at work from man at play or any other of his activities. In the wider sense of man's 'life-space', in the totality of his existence, money could be seen as assuming not only the role of a goal-object, but also serving as a pathway leading towards greater satisfaction out of work or the minimisation of discomfort in his life-style as a whole. There is some contemporary empirical evidence (Goldthorpe, et al., 1968) to suggest that this may be so, and to which we shall refer later. Proposal has also been made that money can become an acquired drive in its own right. When other drives have been satisfied, for which money was *originally* the vehicle, people will still seek money. Evidence is contentious, based on research into acquired drives with animals. Maybe money does gain some importance from its association with other stimuli, through its pairing with other primary rewards, according to stimulus-response theory. The incentive power of money as a secondary reinforcer can be maintained even when the primary reward is removed. But, in the words of Opsahl and Dunnette (1966), 'evidence in support of money as a generalised conditioned reinforcer is, at best, limited and inconclusive'. The further proposition has been put forward (Dollard and Miller, 1950) that money can become a *specific* conditioned incentive, that is, a *new* learned drive can be established for money when it *later* becomes paired with other (primary) rewards, based on earlier animal experiments, but once again generalisation to mankind is highly tenuous.

31

It is not simply from the point of view of pedagogy that passing reference has been made either to Lewinian field-theory or to drive theory, for they form the roots from which a major theory about the motivational power of money has emerged, namely expectancy theory. Drive theory is the older, and can be traced back to Greek origins and ideas about hedonistic behaviour. Hull (1931, 1943) was the chief protagonist in more modern psychology with his view that biological needs incite activity, and a 'drive' develops to satisfy the need. The strength of the drive is proportional to the degree of deprivation. The theory focuses on stimulus-response connections, which elicit habits in individual behaviour, and build up a certain habit strength. Objects or goals which have the power to reduce the primary drives of an individual can assume the role of secondary reinforcers of behaviour. Drive theory, or reinforcement theory, is therefore very much concerned with past behaviour and associations. Learned behaviour has resulted from pairings in the past with other rewards. In a summary, these ideas about motivation can be expressed as a function of drive × habit.

The stimulus-response school ignore the possibility of instrumentality, an idea taken up by Tolman (1932) (still working with animals), and Lewin (1938) (concerned with humans). Tolman and Lewin laid the foundations of expectancy theory in their hypotheses about human behaviour. The main concepts are that subjective preferences exist for desired goals or outcomes, that subjective probabilities exist in the minds of individuals that certain things can and will be achieved. A degree of expectation exists. Further, individuals have a range of preferences among the outcomes they seek. In some ways, expectancy theory is not purely a psychological theory, but incorporates decision theory, borrowed from economics. One of the fundamental assumptions is that an individual can assign a utility (value, or valence) to a particular goal (outcome, or incentive). Atkinson (1958) began to crystallise these ideas in his proposition that motivation is a function of motivational disposition × incentive × expectation.

However, it was Victor Vroom (1964) who posited the ideas of expectancy theory in the form of a truly cognitive model. For Vroom, money acquires a *valence* (a degree of importance, an affective orientation or preference) according to the way in which an individual perceives it as having power to obtain other goals or satisfy other desires. An individual will have some subjective assessment of the *expectancy* (probability, belief) that money will in fact achieve the desired outcomes. A degree of elasticity can exist in the mind of an individual as to the strength of the valence or expectancy. The valence of any outcome can range from being unitarily positive ($+1$), which means he prefers attaining it, to unitarily negative (-1), which means he would prefer *not* to attain it; or if the valence were zero (0), he would be indifferent. Similarly, expectation can vary from $+1$ (being completely certain that it will happen), to -1 (certain that it will *not* happen), or possibly hold zero probability (neither belief nor disbelief). Valencies and expectancies can exist at any point along the continuum within the extremes $+1$ and -1. The degree to which a person is motivated to do something is a function of the sum of the products of the valencies of all outcomes and strength of expectancies. Which course of action will be adopted will depend on the relative strength of forces. We should make the point that a valence does not, of course, have any intrinsic value in its own right, but acts simply as means to an end. Money, for instance, will have a higher valence according to the number of needs the individual thinks it will satisfy. To this extent, Vroom acknowledges individual differences in motives, values and abilities. For any individual, in a nutshell, valency $\times$ expectancy $=$ outcome.

Vroom is something of an iconoclast. He does not base his theory at all on drives or needs. Rather he attempts, in retrospect, to mould his model on historical research findings concerning occupational choice, job satisfaction and levels of job performance. The theory is diagnostic rather than prognostic. Unfortunately, the crucial link between the intensity of motivation and the actual, overt performance which ensues, is undefined and undemonstrated. He does not translate motivation into performance. He leaves this question unanswered, mainly because he does not answer the prior and more fundamental question of how in fact outcomes assume a valence in the first place. What Vroom does offer is some idea, perhaps in a rather nebulous form, that the level of performance varies directly with an individual's need for achievement and anticipated satisfaction from an outcome (a theme taken up by Lawler and Porter) and the notion that performance is higher if individuals believe they are overcompensated (contradicted by Jaques). One of the repercussions which is bound to crop up in this type of retrospective model building derives from the fact that personality differences have played a less than significant part in research on job satisfaction. It is all very well, but not enough, to say that job satisfaction reflects the valence of a job to its occupant, and is a result of his perception of the situation and personality constructs.

Vroom emphasised the concepts of valency, expectancy and force, and his thinking is clearly influenced by Lewin. Brief mention ought also to be made of some ideas stimulated by Georgopoulos, Mahoney and Jones (1957) who postulated that productivity is a function of one's motivation to perform at a given level, and that motivation itself depends on the strength of individual needs and the perceived utility of various individual behaviours to achieve various goals. Both Vroom and Georgopoulos *et al.* influenced Lawler and Porter (1967) in their formulation of a more comprehensive motivational model. There is considerable agreement between Vroom and Lawler and Porter, although some difference in terminology. For Lawler and Porter, motivated behaviour is a function of hedonism, in other words, things which have been found satisfying in the past tend to be repeated in the future; and also of expectancy, in other words what one does will depend on what one expects to get out of it, without necessarily having experienced it before. Essentially, two ratios exist in the minds of individuals: on the one hand effort and reward; and on the other, effort and performance and accordingly an individual will move into a state of equilibrium in the balance between the two ratios. It is perhaps easier to explain the model diagrammatically than verbally (Fig. 2.1). The theory states that the degree of effort expended will depend upon the way in which an individual assesses the value or attractiveness of rewards as purveyors of satisfaction. Lawler and Porter lay stress particularly on the Maslovian values of security, esteem, autonomy and self-actualisation. Values may not be constant, but may change over time. Effort depends, in addition, upon the belief or expectancy that the rewards to be obtained are in fact in some way related to that degree of effort expended, and not to some other arbitrary criteria. Effort also depends on the probability that performance will be recognised and rewarded accordingly. Measurement of reward values, effort and performance in quantitative terms is difficult. The whole process is highly subjective. The emphasis is on an individual's *perceived* probabilities and not on *actual* probabilities. Effort is further modified by one's capacities and inclinations and by the perception of one's work role. But the basic hypothesis remains: 'the greater the value of a set of rewards and the higher the probability that

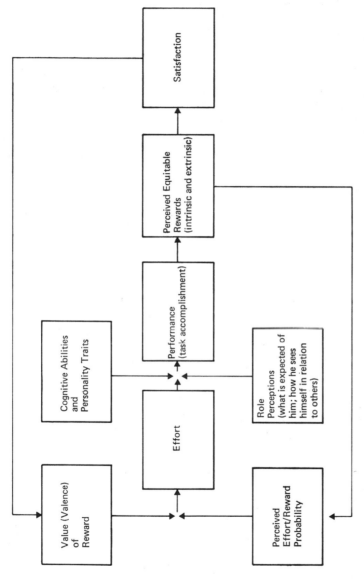

Fig. 2.1 Adaptation of the Theoretical Model Presented by Lawler and Porter (1967) and Lawler (1971)

receiving each of these rewards depends upon effort, the greater the effort that will be put forth in a given situation' (Lawler and Porter, 1967). The underlying construct of need-path(effort)-goal(rewards) is clearly Lewinian. The model can be criticised for its instrumentality. People do not always act logically and rationally in their pursuit of goals, but no model of motivation can be perfect. No model can have general and universal validity so long as individual differences exist between people. In a nutshell, Lawler and Porter's model states that effective motivation (effort) = sum of reward value × perceived probability that effort leads to reward.

What we have now reached at this stage of our development of motivational theory is some acknowledgement that money is important. There has been a swing back in recent years to the view that money *is* a motivational factor at work, and that it must be fair and equitable, with due regard to the effort expended, skills required, levels of responsibility and so on. How we might achieve the optimum distribution of money for work is the subject matter for the greater part of this book. Meanwhile, apart from recent hypothetical models, there is contemporary empirical evidence that people sometimes do adopt calculative attitudes to work. For example, Goldthorpe and his colleagues (Goldthorpe, Lockwood, Bechhofer, Platt, 1968), in a study of the critical incidents affecting the occupational decisions of workers taking up employment in the Vauxhall plant at Luton, discovered that the prime reason why workers had vacated previously held employment in jobs of high intrinsic satisfaction in favour of routine, repetitive work on a car assembly line was because they saw work first and foremost as a source of income which they sought to maximise. Money was rated higher than recognition, acceptance by peers, appreciation of supervisors. Indeed, they adopted a highly insular, instrumental attitude both in their work and outside it. This may be an extreme case. W. W. Daniel (1970) has suggested in a Herzbergian sort of way that the interests and aspirations of people at work vary according to the situation and the work environment. At one time their attentions may well focus on the job context, on negotiations about wages, salaries, security, manpower establishments, but only when there are strong external motivations to do so, such as what other people may be earning, fear of lay-off, shortage of alternative work and so on. At other times, they will be very much concerned with job content, with the work itself, and their intrinsic needs.

36

The situation is never static, and so policy definition is never easy.

In the long run the success of any payment system depends on how well it is accepted by the population it serves. What is felt in terms of satisfaction with pay depends in turn on how an individual perceives it as a fair and just reward in relation to the effort he has to put forth in harnessing his physical, cognitive and conative abilities in order to do the job successfully, and in relation to what he sees other people earning in return for their own skills and efforts. Elliott Jaques in recent years has tackled these fundamental issues, and has developed the concepts of Homans' 'distributive justice' (1951, 1961) and Adams' 'equity theory' (1963, 1965), a derivative of Festinger's 'cognitive dissonance theory' (1957), into a theoretical system for equitable payment. The concept of equity rests on an individual's perceived balance between his inputs and outputs. The situation, as perceived, may not necessarily correspond to reality. The crux of the issue is the relationship which an individual sees in his own input-output balance *vis-à-vis* other people's. In equity theory, cognitive dissonance can arise if imbalance exists in the ratio between an individual's inputs into work (his age, education, experience, skills and efforts) and his outputs (pay, fringe benefits, job satisfaction, status, freedom). Individuals move towards equilibrium in the ratio, either by varying their input contribution, or by changing their outputs, for example making alterations in their comparative reference group, moving to a higher paid job, or by complete withdrawal from the situation. Dissonance creates tension in direct proportion to the degree of inequity. Normally dissonance must lead to action, since a drive is created to reduce the feelings of inequity. Overpayment and underpayment can both give rise to feelings of inequity. There are a variety of possible ways in which the matter may be resolved, and the actual outcome will depend on an individual's perception of the implied causal connection between inputs and outputs. Jaques' solution to the elimination of dissonance rests on a payment system in which jobs are evaluated according to norms of equity, a system for equitable payment based on people's intuitive feelings for 'felt-fair pay'. Rather than evaluate jobs in terms of their inputs which has been the conventional approach for deciding pay, and which because of their subjective measurement may invariably be incorrect or even inappropriate, hence giving rise to feelings of unfairness resolvable only through power politics drawing forth the baser instincts of man, Jaques advocates a common criterion. For Jaques the important element of work is that which has discretionary content rather than that which is prescribed by laid-down rules and procedures. The amount of discretion called for in a work role is a variable of which the overt effects are to a greater or lesser extent delayed. The longer the period of time which can elapse before sub-standard discretion becomes evident (the time-span of discretion) then the greater the level of responsibility inherent in the job and correspondingly the greater the financial reward normally deemed appropriate. From his researches Jaques has observed that people have an unconscious awareness of the monetary worth of jobs. A set of normative values exists which comes to light during 'social-analytical' interviews. These norms correlate with the time-span of discretion. Therefore, the theory goes, if time-span can be measured, one has the key to a system for equitable payment which has universal applicability, prevents social injustice and eliminates states of tension arising from imbalance in the ratio of pay and level of work. The theory has obvious and important implications both for a discussion of social and psychological attitudes to pay and for practical policy. Presented here is just an outline, but a full appraisal of his treatment, its practicality and the controversy it has generated is given in Chapter 6.

The behaviour of man is exceedingly complex. What motivates him has been a matter of prolonged and absorbing interest. The answers are far from clear. The psychological theories which have been put forward are largely products of their time. The models which have been presented do not have universal validity; they contain an element of truth and an element of error. So wide is the range of individual differences and human aspirations, so variable are the goals and the means by which they are sought, that a master plan is likely to remain elusive. The values attached to money as a reward for effort will vary from man to man. In modern industrial society, money forms part of the contract for work. One thing is certain. Whatever its relative importance, the rate for the job must at least be got right. Job evaluation is a means to that end.

Chapter 3

Preparing the Groundwork for Job Evaluation

It is not uncommon nowadays to think of organisational activity in general, and industrial activity in particular, as a process of conversion of various inputs into a system into appropriate outputs. The conversion process involves an optimum combination of inputs like capital, land, human effort, raw materials, entrepreneurial risk and so on set to work to produce a desired outcome. The element of human effort is an integral part of this activity, but one which we must isolate in order to assess the value of its particular contribution. For the wage and salary earner it is simply regarded as 'work'. The *Concise Oxford Dictionary* (1970) defines work variously as 'expenditure of energy, striving, application of effort to some purpose', 'Task (to be) undertaken' and 'employment, especially the opportunity of earning money'. Our last definition contains the nub of a number of problems, for which the techniques of job evaluation offer some solution. To measure the expenditure of human effort and its resultant pay-off to an organisation is by no means easy. As jobs become more complex, so the problem becomes more intractable. Job evaluation itself is an incomplete tool; it is only an aid towards a rational consideration of the more important differences between the inputs of human contribution in jobs. It seeks to highlight significant disparities between units of work on a comparative basis, and so produce a more equitable distribution of income within an organisation than might be obtained by more arbitrary methods.

Job evaluation itself is in fact a generic term for a number of techniques which by applying common criteria to job assessment enable a logical, equitable and acceptable structure to be formed. Much of course depends on one's interpretation of such concepts as equity and acceptability, but it should be apparent that assessment against uniform standards on the basis of consensus between the parties concerned, i.e. employers and employees, should on the face of it produce a greater system of social justice than, say, autocratic rule-of-thumb decisions, favouritism or a blatant display of relative bargaining power. It is worth quoting the British Institute of Management's (1970) definition of job evaluation as 'the process of analysing and assessing the content of jobs, in order to place them in an acceptable rank order which can then be used as a basis for a remuneration system. Job evaluation, therefore, is simply a technique designed to assist in the development of new pay structures by defining relativities between jobs on a consistent and systematic basis.' In other words, job evaluation is ultimately concerned with the rate for the job. The techniques are confined to the scope and importance of the work itself.

In its pure form, job evaluation eschews the contribution of an individual job incumbent in terms of his or her performance, potential or personal qualities. Some of the criticisms which have been levelled against job evaluation are that it is, therefore, impersonal, that it concentrates on measuring the inputs into a task rather than the outputs, and that it can only form part of the basis of a policy for remuneration. True, it only forms part of the parcel. To it must be added adequate monetary rewards and incentives for individual performance or merit, compensations for seniority of services or some supplementary mechanism to overcome market scarcity factors.

The apotheosis of job evaluation as a panacea or some divine device for the solution of pay problems is both wrong and misleading. It is no more than a formula for fairness. Its limitations should be realised from the outset. The implications are that a much wider view must be taken of a personnel pay policy. These issues are taken up in Chapter 9. The purpose of job evaluation is to arrange for an equitable disbursement of available wealth within the constraints of the overriding criteria of company profitability, willingness to pay, prevailing market forces, and the sort of compensation policy an organisation wishes to see emerge. Job evaluation is but one thread in the total fabric; it is part of the complex interaction of variables; its precise contribution sometimes becomes difficult to disentangle from the web of business strategy, constraints and politics. More Machiavellian commentators have regarded it as an instrument for economic exploitation and political domination. Unfortunately, the truth of these allegations is sometimes easy to find. The success or otherwise of job evaluation depends like most things on the way in which it is implemented. In an autocratic, dictatorial environment it can be made to produce one thing; in an open, democratic environment it can be made to produce quite another. In the one case antagonism, hostility and suspicion will be the pay-off; in the other, a workable basis for constructive negotiation and discussion can be the elusive prize. No one could deny that its contribution is not incomplete. 'Job evaluation is no patented formula for the cure of all industrial relations and wage determination ills' (Patton, Littlefield, Self, 1964). It can only provide a skeleton framework for building a system of equitable payment, but that framework itself will be denied the organisation which does not attempt to found its pay policy upon consensus.

The objective of job evaluation has been defined as a method to determine the relative differences between jobs in terms of job content, and so one immediately comes up against the problem of measurement. The origins of the analytical study of work go back to Babbage in the early nineteenth century, and to the work of later pioneers such as Taylor, the Gilbreths, and Bedaux in the early part of this century. From their studies the three management techniques of method study (motion study), work measurement and job evaluation have emerged. Job evaluation is the youngest of the trilogy, and is in many ways quite distinct and separate, although it stems from a common root. The point to be made is that the evaluation of jobs can only begin with a careful study or analysis of their contents. Job analysis is a fundamental prerequisite of job evaluation.

It should be emphasised that job evaluation is not an end in itself. Indeed, it lacks utility from the point of view of the enterprise or the people in it, unless the information obtained and conclusions drawn can be translated into prices. Pricing of jobs is very much concerned with differentials according to job worth, but this segment of the problem cannot be taken out of context of the overall wage and salary bill. The total payroll cost is of critical importance. Whilst by definition, job evaluation is concerned with relativities, by implication and by extrapolation its application must also be linked with the determination of absolutes. Job evaluation is a means to an end. For that reason considerable attention is paid to the actual pricing of structures which result from the conventional techniques explained in detail in the next chapters. It would be unwise to embark upon a consideration of the essential groundwork if we were to lose sight of our final goal or end product. However, our immediate task is to focus on foundations: the need for consensus and job analysis.

CONSENSUS

Right at the outset, from the very first preliminary discussions about the distribution of corporate wealth, removal of pay anomalies, or possible introduction of job evaluation, paramount attention ought to be given to prime issues, namely the objectives to be achieved and the formulation of a successful policy for achieving them. Simply stated, this sounds no more than common sense, almost a tautology. Yet too large a number of plans to introduce job evaluation founder or are stillborn because these fundamental questions get short shrift, or are even unasked and unanswered. The cause, most frequently, is a unitary view taken of the organisational system by management. Management prerogatives and conventional ideas about authority die hard. As Alan Fox (1966) has pointed out, industrial life is more appropriately viewed as a 'pluralistic' system consisting of various vested interests. Behavioural scientists have repeatedly indicated that the objectives of employers are not necessarily the same as those of employees. Where incompatibility exists, resistance will be manifest. Conflict is endemic. In the words of Gordon Lippitt (1969), 'conflict releases energy at every level of human affairs—energy that can produce positive, constructive results. Two things should be recognised here. First, that such conflict is an absolutely predictable social phenomenon. Second, that conflict should not be repressed, but channelled to useful purposes.' The portents of the behavioural sciences are that a participative approach is called for. Participation is a broad concept, and can be defined to mean different aspects and intensities of industrial democracy, but always signifying the involvement of work-people, to a greater or lesser extent, in decision making.

Certainly an authoritarian, autocratic approach, to such a sensitive issue as pay, is an invitation to trouble, truculence and sabotage. Viteles (1954), surveying the results of research in the field of worker-management participation, concludes 'that *employee participation in decision-*

making, in a *democratic atmosphere* created by "permissive" leadership, facilitates the development of "internalised" motivation, and serves to raise the levels of employee production and morale'. Again, another noted behavioural scientist, Vroom (1968), comes to a similar conclusion. He writes: 'The results suggest that allocating problem-solving and decision-making tasks to entire work-groups, as compared with the leader or manager in charge of the groups, requires a greater investment of man-hours but produces higher acceptance of decisions and a higher probability that the decisions will be executed efficiently.' The point to be made is that the people affected should be involved at the very inception of any plans to introduce change or systematise an existing situation. Failure to do so will only imperil success. Indeed, the concurrence of work-people is required as to whether job evaluation should be used at all. Not until then does it become apposite to debate the relative merits, demerits and relevance of a particular scheme to a given situation and possible ways of implementing it. Consultative machinery for securing the right environment, commitment and co-operation needs careful thought, whether or not trade unions are involved or whether some form of representative committee is set up on a purely internal basis as obtains for large sections of white-collar employment.

Processes of decision making are highly complex. Acceptability is but one aspect of a number of interrelationships. Consensus must be reached in principle on the objective in hand. This is only the beginning. In the ensuing discussions, the process of reaching agreement or compromise becomes extremely deep, influenced by both rational and emotional factors. Decisions made in committees or other joint negotiating bodies are probably the most complex of all, where a number of people acting either from individual motives or in the interest of the parties they represent, bring to the meeting a cosmos of interacting attitudes, opinions and aspirations ranging from economic and social, to power, prestige and status. Decisions made in committee generally take longer to reach, although there is some tentative evidence to suggest that their 'quality' may be better. The temptation may well be there for management to uphold its prerogative, issue an edict and decree the introduction of such and such a job evaluation scheme. 'Scientific management, from its early developments in time and motion study to its contemporary manifestations in linear and heuristic programming, has contributed to the centralisation of decision making in organisations by focusing on the development of methods by which managers can make more rational decisions, substituting objective measurements and empirically validated methods for causal judgments' (Vroom, 1968).

In a technological and competitive age, involving high degrees of know-how, risk-taking and capital investment, there are clearly in certain areas some decisions which can only be taken at the highest level. But we are considering the day-to-day working conditions of workfolk. We are dealing with people, not robots. Few would deny that it is sometimes politically advantageous to 'juggle' the results of a job evaluation scheme in order to reach consensus, rather than aim at scientific accuracy. If people do not accept the outcome, it will not work anyway. It is as well to remember the moral of Elton Mayo (Chapter 2) who first drew attention to the organisation as a social system rather than an economic one, and who emphasised that the critical element in organisational life was co-operation.

Before considering any of the techniques of job evaluation in detail it is not only advisable, but vital, to ascertain whether the idea is acceptable in principle, and to ensure that people have not only a voice but a positive influence in the way in which it is set up. Some plural body, perhaps called a job evaluation committee, will need to review all the jobs under consideration. The final outcome of their deliberations, and job ratings produced, is really a measure of consensus reached in committee. The constitution of the committee, therefore, is important and merits careful thought and planning. The problem of its size can be a tricky one. Too large a committee becomes unmanageable, but it should at least provide room for adequate representation of the various interested parties. The number of jobs to be evaluated will also be a factor, for it is unreasonable to burden too small a committee with an excessive volume of work. There are no hard and fast rules that apply. As a general guideline, the very smallest committee, evaluating no more than, say, 100 jobs, should not have a membership strength of less than half a dozen. Such a group might usefully comprise representatives from employees whose jobs are to be evaluated, representatives from line management selected for their intimate knowledge of the organisation and jobs in question, and one or two representatives from the personnel department whose main role will be one of co-ordination, administration and follow-up. With larger numbers of jobs, more people will have to be brought in. In very large organisations, or where extensive job evaluation is contemplated, it might be more feasible to have a central co-ordinating committee with a number of sub-committees to consider particular divisions of the company or particular geographical locations in multi-site operations.

JOB ANALYSIS

The starting point for any scheme of job evaluation is to obtain knowledge about the jobs concerned, in order that comparative decisions may be made about them. It would be true to say that all personnel work requires as much information about jobs as it does about people, and in the case of job evaluation, the emphasis centres quite squarely on the nature and content of the work itself, rather than the people doing it. Job analysis, a fundamental tool of personnel management, is a process of investigation into the activities of work and the demands made upon workers, irrespective of the type or level of employment. H. E. Roff and T. E. Watson (1961) of Management Selection Services Ltd state: 'The process of analysing a job is essentially one of determining its major characteristics or dimensions.' It is an analysis of the job we are concerned with, not the incumbent. There is nothing new about job analysis, and for many years people from professions relevant to the study of man at work have tackled it from various angles. Engineers, for instance, have tended to concentrate on the physical aspects of the job, on the working environment. Psychologists have focused their attention on the capacities and inclinations which a job calls for in a person in order that it should be performed satisfactorily.

The uses to which the results of job analysis can be put are wide and far-reaching: personnel recruitment and selection, the identification of training needs, definition of training programmes, organisation and manpower planning, job evaluation, the design of equipment and methods of work—more or less the whole range of personnel activities. An interesting study by Zerga (1943) listed some twenty uses for the information obtained from job analysis. Put another way, job analysis is a starting point for almost any occupational problem. To some extent this confuses the issue. The amount of detail, presentation of information and the critical items of information about a job need not be the same whatever the results of job analysis are used for. The purpose for

45

which the information is required must always be borne in mind when facts about the job are assembled and recorded. For instance, the important details of a job which are used as the basis for a job specification in personnel selection may have a different emphasis from those which are of particular significance for job evaluation.

At this point it may be helpful to clarify and define some of the terminology to be found in the literature, and used subsequently in this book. Job analysis has already been defined. Two related terms are those of *job description* and *job specification*. These terms are sometimes used indiscriminately, but for our purposes job description can be regarded as a written statement of the main duties and responsibilities which a job entails, and job specification (or 'man specification') as a list of criteria in terms of the personal capacities and inclinations deemed necessary for successful job performance. It might further be useful to distinguish between *jobs* and *tasks*. Basically, tasks are the component elements in a work role which have to be accomplished, the various bits of work which together make up the whole job. A job, therefore, is the composition of all those activities performed by a single person, which can be regarded as a unified concept, and which finds a formal place in the organisation chart.

Despite the subtle difference in interpretation given to the result of job analysis according to its end purpose, the basic process of eliciting information is common. Roff and Watson (1961) suggests two stages: '(1) to collect and record evidence of the nature of the job; (2) to sift this recorded data to discover those aspects of the job which are important in relation to the problems which have prompted the undertaking of the job analysis'. Most important is the need to gain the trust, confidence and co-operation of those whose jobs are being placed under scrutiny. The job analyst is naturally regarded with suspicion. Where his investigations are going to be used as the basis for job evaluation, it would be easy for him to be regarded as an enemy, in the knowledge that his reports could lead to an undermining of an individual's status, relative pay and organisational position. Tact and diplomacy are called for, and this is easier said than done. The general observations which we made in considering the whole problem of consensus and participation again become relevant. Good communication is essential. People should be elucidated as to the purpose of the exercise, the reasons why it is necessary, what it is hoped will be achieved, ways in which the information obtained will be collated and processed, and how decisions affecting their jobs will be arrived at. Better still would it be for them to be invited either directly or through representatives to contribute to the formation of that policy and its execution. Constraints imposed by the sheer size of the organisation and volume of work to be done severely limit the degree of discussion and participation which is possible, but every effort should be made to see that all contentions are aired, suspicions displaced and uncertainties answered. It is clearly only within an atmosphere of trust and co-operation that truthful and constructive relations between job incumbent and job analyst can be achieved. With anything less, the results will be contaminated, distorted and, most probably, quite invalid.

Sifting the important from the trivial aspects of a job during and after the analysis is really what the whole exercise is about. Attention finally should be directed at the significant differences between jobs, having first collected all the relevant information necessary to form a complete picture of any particular unit of work. There are no hard and fast rules that can be applied; at root it is a matter of judgement. A common danger is to collect too much information, making it difficult to see the wood from the trees. On the whole this is a more common pitfall than making just a cursory examination and ending up with a sketchy, incomplete picture. In making the analysis, if a fact is unimportant, it should immediately be discarded. To provide a framework on which to structure both the analysis and the information obtained, it is useful to look at the job from two points of view: first, the duties and responsibilities entailed; second, the skills and personal attributes necessary for the successful execution of that job. What we are really saying is that information can be collected and presented in a way which fits in with general personnel practice, namely in the twin form of a job description and job specification. Although some may quibble with this two-edged approach, the overriding consideration is that the outcome be presented in a standard format, to facilitate comparison between jobs. Treating the two complementary aspects of job analysis in tandem does, in the experience of the author, provide two clear and practical starting points, and makes it easier to classify and codify information within natural and logical perimeters. What an individual does and what personal attributes he needs to bring to the job provide us with the dimensions critical for making evaluative decisions between the relative worth of one job and another.

The main steps in the process of job analysis can be set out as follows:

1. Identify and isolate, for the purposes of study, the *component tasks* in a job. (Some jobs may consist of a large number of tasks and sub-tasks, and it may be convenient to group some of these into task 'taxonomies' where there is sufficient in common between them, to reduce the complexity of the analysis to manageable proportions.)

2. Examine *how* tasks are performed (e.g. the skills required; order in which they have to be exercised; whether tasks are done in isolation or as part of a team effort, etc.).

3. Examine *why* tasks are performed as they are (why the production or administrative processes concerned require these various inputs; the relationship of tasks to each other within a job and to other jobs in the organisation).

4. Examine *when* and *why* tasks are performed (to complete the operational picture).

5. (*a*) Identify the *main duties* involved, both regular and occasional.
   (*b*) Scale the main duties according to their difficulty, frequency and importance to the job as a whole.

6. Identify the main areas of *responsibility* (e.g. responsibility for various assignments of work; responsibility for the work of other people; responsibilities for money, plant and equipment, materials, turnover, etc.). Where it is possible to quantify these aspects of a job, so much the better.

7. Note the prevailing *working conditions*, in respect of the physical, social and financial aspects of the job.
   (*a*) Physical environment (temperature, noise, dirt, danger, or comfortable office facilities, etc.).
   (*b*) Social environment (whether in teams, shifts, isolated work, etc.).
   (*c*) Financial conditions. (If a payment system is already in existence, note the basic wage rate or salary currently obtaining, and any bonus, incentive schemes, fringe benefits, etc., which may apply.)

8. Identify the *personal demands* which a job makes on an individual incumbent. (NB—this is not a description of the attributes which the

present incumbent happens to possess, but a breakdown of those essential attributes which are deemed necessary for successful performance, and without which it would not be possible to do the job properly). Demands can be categorised according to the following criteria:

(a) Physical demands (e.g. muscular energy, sedentary work, travel, hours of work, appearance, bearing, speech, any basic medical requirements, etc.).

(b) Intellectual demands. In general terms we may consider whether a university degree, HNC, 'O' levels, some technical or professional qualification is necessary, or we may simply note that the job requires 'average' or 'below average' intelligence, etc. The amount of detail recorded under this sub-heading, as any other, will depend on the type of job evaluation scheme to be applied. As we shall see, it may accordingly be more appropriate to consider intellectual inputs in such terms as 'problem-solving' abilities. Note should also be made of any specific intellectual demands, e.g. verbal or numerical ability.

(c) Skills (e.g. any particular psycho-motor, social or diplomatic skills called for).

(d) Experience. Some jobs call for considerable occupational experience, know-how or previously held levels of responsibility, control or decision making. Sometimes it is possible to quantify this factor in terms of a given number of years. More frequently such quantifications are misleading, for they can only be arrived at somewhat arbitrarily or by reference to the present incumbent's own personal history. At least, where previous experience in certain areas is essential, these should be identified and specified in terms of levels and depth rather than numbers of years.

(e) Personality factors (e.g. such things called for in the job as the ability to work through other people, to provide leadership, to initiate, to work without close supervision, to possess a degree of extraversion, or the kind of temperament to cope with dull, routine procedures, etc.).

Approached in this way a complete overview of the job can be built up. Standardisation facilitates the drawing up of a job information sheet which can provide a workable and acceptable basis for comparisons to be made. There are, of course, very many different ways in

49

which job analysis can be tackled. Items 1–7 above cover the information which would normally go into a job description, and the topics under item 8 cover the main points of a job specification. The suggestion here is that a comprehensive job information sheet be compiled for each job. It does not matter whether it is called a job description or job specification, provided all relevant information about the job is recorded clearly, accurately, and so far as is possible, with brevity. There are various ways in which information can be obtained. The main methods are as follows:

1. Interviews

Probably the most flexible and productive approach is for the job analyst to conduct a personal interview with the job holder. Properly structured, the interview can elicit information about all aspects of the job, the nature and sequence of the various component tasks, the whys and wherefores. Some appraisal can be made of the skills required for doing it. It is useful to cross-check the information obtained with incumbents of identical or similar jobs, to highlight any discrepancies in reporting, and furthermore, to consult with the immediate supervisor on the final outcome with a view to validating the accuracy, balance and inferences relating to the details obtained. The rapport which can be obtained in face-to-face interaction between analyst and employee can do much to dispel any doubts and suspicions which might be held. Occasionally one comes across the recalcitrant, obstructive job-holder— but that is all in a day's work!

2. Observation

Some jobs lend themselves to direct observation, particularly routine jobs with a high manual content, where much of the job activity is there for the eye to see, and where not too much is hidden in the form of mental processes or in the exercise of individual discretion. It is unlikely that simple observation will produce all the answers, but it can always be backed up with interview and discussion.

3. Activity Sampling

This is really a more sophisticated development of the simple observation method reported above. In activity sampling a large number of observations are taken at random intervals during the complete working cycle. The purpose of each observation is to snap-shot what the job holder is actually doing, and at the end of the period, which might last some days or weeks, to express the number of times an activity occurs as a percentage of the total number of observations made, in order to arrive at the relative importance or frequency of various visible outputs. It is a technique which, on the whole, is more favoured by work-study men than by personnel officers, and is unlikely to provide all the information required without the backing of interview and discussion, and is in any case more applicable where job performance is overt.

4. *Questionnaires*
With a large number of similar jobs of a routine clerical nature, it may well be expeditious and time-saving to structure a questionnaire to be circulated to all employees in those jobs. The questionnaire must, of course, be tailor-made to elicit the right sort of responses and useful information. A prerequisite is to interview at least one incumbent, and the boss too, to get a feel of the job in order to ask pertinent questions. The replies can then be sorted, and any further details, misunderstandings, gaps or disagreements can be investigated during the interview.

5. *Critical Incidents*
The critical incident technique (Flanagan, 1954) is an attempt to identify the more important, or 'noteworthy', aspects of job behaviour. Originally it was developed as a check-list rating procedure for performance appraisal, but its merits lend itself to other investigatory activities such as job analysis for the purpose of job evaluation. In this latter context, the idea is to highlight the critical aspects of a job which are crucial to its successful performance. It can usefully be applied to multitask jobs as a means for establishing priorities between job elements. First, the critical incidents must be identified, and second, scaled in order of their difficulty, frequency, importance or contribution to the job as a whole. Although it is helpful to pinpoint critical incidents, an analysis constructed in this way will not provide a complete and integrated picture of the whole job.

6. *Diaries*
This method is a self-reporting analysis of the activities engaged in over a period and the amount of time spent on all of them, recorded in the

form of a diary. It can become tedious and onerous for the job incumbent, and is probably the method most open to abuse and faking. Although it can provide a synopsis of the activities actually engaged in, it cannot provide very much hard data about the skills or expertise deployed.

The process of job analysis is much more difficult than might appear at first sight. The conventional techniques listed all have their limitations. For managerial jobs, the matter can become very complicated, and it may well be necessary to construct the analysis in terms of the criteria by which the job is to be evaluated, e.g. problem-solving, accountability, know-how. Moreover, jobs are not constant, but change over time, and they are influenced in no small measure by the personality, drive and enthusiasm of the people doing them. Job analysis can be misleading, almost a diversion, for it is the synthesis of the various inputs which really make for success, and for which a firm is paying. The totality of a job is greater than the sum of its individual parts. As in all stages in job evaluation, the evidence should be treated with caution.

Chapter 4

Applying Conventional Job Evaluation Techniques—Non-Quantitative

Strictly speaking, job evaluation is concerned to determine the relative position of one job to another. It is a preliminary exercise for the establishment of grades and associated wage and salary levels. In the next two chapters we shall follow the exercises through to their logical conclusion. Conventionally, four main techniques have been developed: the cruder, simpler non-quantitative methods of *ranking* and *classification* and the more sophisticated quantitative methods of *points rating* and *factor comparison*. We begin with the non-quantitative techniques.

RANKING

Administratively, job ranking is probably the easiest scheme to conduct. It does not call for overmuch detail in job analysis and it can be executed relatively quickly with a minimum of expenditure of time, energy and resources. Although producing a structure which is not finely discriminating, it does provide an acceptable basis for discussion and negotiation. It is non-analytical in the sense that jobs are not broken down into their component elements and requirements for careful appraisal and comparison, but instead, are compared as 'wholes'. It is non-quantitative in the sense that it does not give any indication of the *degree* of difference between jobs, but simply indicates whether one job is more or less demanding of an individual or more or less important to the organisation than another. As the name implies, it produces a rank order of jobs.

The first step is analysis. By one of the methods indicated in Chapter 3, information about the jobs must be assembled and recorded in a standard format. It is important to remember that the objective of the exercise is to rank the jobs and not the incumbents. In practice it is sometimes difficult not to be swayed by the personality and performance of the man doing it rather than the work itself. For this reason, carefully prepared job analysis information is essential. A job evaluation committee, the constitution and functions of which have previously been discussed, will need to be set up to review the jobs under consideration.

The easiest way to structure the operation is to begin with the identification of *key job* or *bench mark jobs*. A bench mark job is one which will be used as a yardstick and as a standard against which other jobs will be compared from an overall point of view. Definition and clarification of key jobs is a central issue. A bench mark job is no use if there is disagreement about its content, demands or relative importance. It should be exscinded if the slightest controversy exists. Preferably it should be one which represents a wide range of job requirements. All assessors must be thoroughly acquainted with the elements of work, skill and effort involved in it. Having ensured this general provision, bench mark jobs should be selected at various levels in the organisation or existing hierarchy. Obviously there must be clear differentiation between bench mark jobs to start with. Too many of them can well confuse the issue, whilst too few will provide inadequate dispersion of anchorage points to act as a workable framework or skeleton.

Bench mark jobs having been determined, other jobs can be compared against them on an overall basis by asking the question, is this job relatively more important than a bench mark job, or less important? and then placing the job in rank order above or below it according to the answer. Bench mark jobs therefore act as focal points around which other jobs are clustered. The selection and deployment of bench mark jobs does to some extent prejudge the outcome, because one is required to make some decision as to which would be the most appropriate one in the as yet ill-defined hierarchy to compare a job with. Once the original purpose as a focus has been served, a bench mark job begins to lose its utility as ranking progresses, until it eventually may become redundant. When a partial hierarchical outline begins to emerge, ranking requires as much comparison to be made against jobs which have already been placed as it does against bench mark jobs. Kick-off points are proffered by bench mark jobs, but it may subsequently be easier and more accurate to rank jobs against others which have already been placed in the emerging structure.

To simplify the process of comparison with unwieldy numbers of jobs, common practice (as advocated by the British Institute of Management) is to reduce the job analysis information or job description to specially prepared cards, ideally so that all the relevant details are presented on one side in as concise a manner as possible. Cards can then be shuffled backwards and forwards on a trial and error basis, judging the jobs according to their importance to the organisation and the demands they make on the job holder. This facility increases the number of jobs which any assessor can conveniently handle.

Problems are more acute in large organisations, where the prospects may be quite daunting. If across-the-board job evaluation is to be applied, a points system may be better. However, there are ways of getting to grips with large-scale ranking. One is to treat functional divisions or 'job families' separately—i.e. to consider accountants, computer personnel or salesmen, etc., as occupational groups without specific reference to the enterprise at large. Since pay must finally reflect differentials in scarcity and skill as between occupations, there may well be some merit in doing it this way. Another is to adopt the techniques of *paired comparison*. By this method each assessor ranks each job in turn against all the others to be evaluated, so that a series of paired rankings is produced. The advantage is that it ensures that every job is considered on a comparative and individual basis with every other job and not just with bench mark jobs. It is a more comprehensive approach, and a logical and methodical way of improving the reliability in rankings even with disparate jobs. The snag is that it is exceedingly cumbersome, and the degree to which it is time-consuming increases proportionately with size. Moreover, there is the problem of achieving consensus between the assessors; the more there are the more difficult it becomes. Obviously eccentric decisions show up clearly, but there are likely to be a number of areas where minor disagreement exists and which despite cajolery remain persistently irresolvable. A high level of consensus between assessors is clearly desirable. One may have to accept a consensus correlation co-efficient of less than unity, but one should certainly not tolerate less than 0·75. One of the newer schemes of job evaluation, the *direct consensus* method (Chapter 6), which utilises a points system on the basis of consensual agreement between assessors, becomes so complicated in both its administration and arithmetic calculations that a computer programme is necessary to resolve the issue.

In small firms the problems, both from the point of view of administration and from the point of view of being able to make sound,
competent judgements as between jobs, may not be so acute. Apart
from a smaller aggregate number of jobs, assessors are more likely to
have an intimate knowledge of them and produce more reliable rankings. The whole business of judgement, in any event, is always highly
subjective, and is one of the main criticisms of the technique. There are
always conflicting ideals imposed by the constraints of business life.
One seeks a high degree of reliability and objectivity in a scheme, and
at the same time a minimum of administrative machinery, time and cost
involvement. Frequently these goals are mutually exclusive and some
compromise must be reached. Belcher (1963), as an aid to discriminating
between jobs, advocates selecting a number of factors in a job as a
basis for arriving at ranking decisions, but once one begins to do this
one is in fact operating a vague and rather woolly points system without any tight or clearly defined controls. Goldenberg (1968) has described a single-factor ranking scheme which has proved workable and
acceptable in Canadian National Railways, based on the significant
difference between jobs as measured by their discretionary content.
Although not acknowledged as such, Goldenberg's scheme derives
from the ideas of Elliott Jaques. Goldenberg states:

'Significant Difference is essentially a single-factor ranking method.
The single factor considered is the discretionary content present in each
job relative to other jobs. No attempt is made to measure precisely the
amount of discretionary content. . . . The Significant Difference method,
then, focuses on the major distinction (where one exists) between any
two jobs. The single most important task performed by an employee is
identified and compared with the single most important task performed
by another employee.'

This particular scheme, applied to clerical workers, illustrates the sort
of compromise strategy which can be successfully introduced in
large-scale organisation when one is wary of the non-specific nature
of orthodox ranking, but at the same time does not want to get too
involved in the detailed minutae of more complex schemes.

The above examples, hybrid variations of ranking, are cited to illustrate some of the attempts which have been made to introduce a
measure of rationale and the definition of some criterion as an aid to

decision making. Pure ranking does not include these refinements. Ranking in its basic form simply requires taking a bird's-eye view of a range of jobs and making some perhaps rather perfunctory decisions about their relative worth, from the angle of both vertical and lateral relationships. Although speedy and straightforward, it cannot claim a high degree of accuracy, nor can it produce a scientifically discriminating differential series of jobs in hierarchical order. It is by definition non-analytical and non-quantitative. If greater degrees of precision are sought after, *ipso facto* some other technique is called for. However, it would be negative to condemn or reject it out of hand. Without some attempt at formalising structure the situation is likely to be even more anomalous and haphazard. In any case ranking is only a preliminary to pricing, when all sorts of considerations and constraints become superimposed on the basic structure and many of the finer points relating to the theoretical reliability and validity of the scheme become glossed over.

For pricing purposes it is customary to divide up the series into *grades*, or groups of jobs, for which will be ascertained a *spread of range* of payment within maximal and minimal limits. In the final analysis, the somewhat arbitrary distinctions which must be made between adjacent jobs and other closely related jobs during the ranking part of the exercise become ironed out when they are marshalled into grades. Within a grade there is, to all intents and purposes, no significant difference between the jobs which comprise it.

Referring briefly once more to ranking methodology, jobs are dispersed around key jobs. Many jobs may be regarded as equal, bearing in mind we consider both vertical and lateral comparisons. The result is the sort of picture appearing in Figure 4.1. The structure tends to be pyramidical as per organisational orthodoxy since the interranking of jobs will naturally tend to reflect the *status quo* situation if antecedent relationships were not too much out of alignment. Even if they were, by virtue of deliberate decisions with regard to the intercomparison of jobs on a hierarchical axis, *a fortiori* the same overall structure would emerge. Predominantly more jobs concentrate in the lower echelons. At first sight the situation may appear rather vague. It may simply be that there is very little significant difference between jobs and, of course, nowhere does one get any indication of clear and absolute differences between jobs.

The amorphous miscellany must be reduced to manageable proportions by the creation of groups or grades. Figure 4.2 shows diagrammatically how such an assembly can be achieved by a sideways concertina-like contraction of the pyramid. The precise delineation of a grade demarcation line is largely a matter of convenience to produce grades which are administratively feasible and which conform with broad levels of responsibility in the organisation. Their function is to collect jobs of comparable responsibility into broad bands as a prelude to pricing the structure in monetary terms. Two sometimes thorny

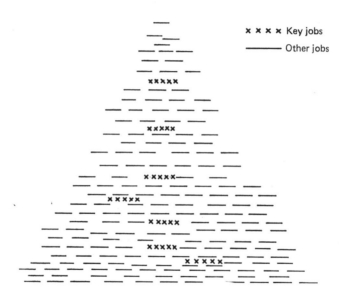

Fig. 4.1   Jobs Ranked around Key Jobs

problems which could have arisen in the ranking are now eliminated by the administrative tactics we have adopted. The first of these concerns the precise differentiation between adjacent jobs. The decision to rank two or more closely allied jobs one above the other is always contentious. It is based on subjective opinion and cannot be validated. What now happens, with grouping, is that all jobs within a grade are regarded as roughly equal and will be priced within the same monetary range. By the same token, problems concerning the differences in relative importance obtaining in two jobs which fall either side of a grade demarcation line can be resolved by the use of *overlap*, a situation where the maximum remuneration of a lower grade extends beyond the minimum point of the next successive grade.

There are no magic formulae for converting the results of a ranking exercise into monetary values. The problem is not peculiar to the

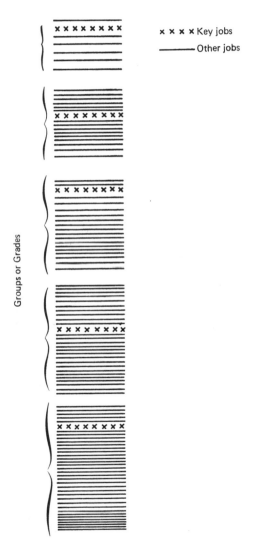

Fig. 4.2   Jobs Assembled for Convenience into Groups or Grades

ranking technique, but obtains for any job evaluation scheme. Indeed, job evaluation as defined is not strictly concerned with this part of the exercise but with relativities. Absolute monetary values depend on the laws of supply and demand for labour as a factor of production, on the purchasing power of the employer, on the scarcity of skills required and so on. One may well ask the question: what contribution does job evaluation have to make if it cannot guide us towards actual values? The answer, and the problem generally, is probably better looked at from the other side of the coin. Monetary values for certain key jobs having already been established, either by reference to prevailing market rates or to wage and salary levels currently obtaining in a firm, job evaluation can guide us towards an equitable relationship and therefore distribution of income between one job and another. If values for certain key jobs can first be established, and the relative differences between jobs be defined in terms of their demands and contribution to the organisation, then we do at least have some indication of what should be the relative differences between jobs in terms of pay.

To price the structure, a number of key jobs must again be determined for which agreement about their appropriate level of pay can be reached. These key jobs do not have to be the same ones as selected for ranking. What is now required is a number of key jobs selected throughout the range, preferably at least one or two in each grade which form clearly defined units of work and for which an agreed rate can be established. There are various ways of doing this. In the UK Civil Service, for example, following the Priestley Royal Commission (1953–5) the Civil Service Pay Research Unit was set up in 1956 as a permanent body which biennially reviews the levels of remuneration, fringe benefits, etc., which obtain for comparable jobs in industry and the private sector. The aim is to ascertain for any specific job a set of rates 'representative of the community as a whole'. This is the essence of a wage and salary survey. The director of the unit has expressed the view that 'if organisations have job evaluation systems, well written job descriptions, or a well graded structure the unit's task is made easier' (Morgan, 1973). For information it should be added that the survey does not include non-industrial civil servants and does not extend beyond Assistant Secretary level (in 1973 maximum remuneration £7,276). Above that the Top Salaries Review Body takes over on rather specialised lines. The Civil Service is quoted as an illustration of principle. It should not be assumed that their internal evaluation is based on ranking, for that is not generally the case. The survey is a means for making 'fair comparisons' and is pertinent irrespective of the type of job evaluation adopted. Having determined prevailing rates, and bearing in mind variations in the conditions of work, an organisation is then in a position to get to grips with the formulation of a wage or salary policy. The Civil Service, in this instance, then base their pay levels within the limits of the median and upper quartile as indicated by comparable jobs outside the service. Few organisations in the private sector maintain such a permanent review body, but make *ad hoc* comparisons from time to time. Any personnel manager should try to keep in touch with what is going on in the labour market, with norms relating to wage and salary levels according to age, occupation and level of responsibility. At its simplest an intuitive feeling can be gleaned from a fairly constant perusal of job advertisements appearing in the press and professional journals. In more sophisticated form, many firms, and particularly larger ones, maintain liaison with other organisations, either competitors, suppliers or customers in their own industry or firms of similar size within their locality or in other industries, to compare notes about what they would tend to pay for any given type or level of job. Such reviews are highly confidential and rarely published. The arrangement might take the form of private dialogue between two or more firms, or it might take place on a wider net through an employers' association. Professional organisations frequently include within their ambit certain remuneration studies and can often give advice on prevailing rates for jobs falling within their occupational ambit. Private organisations, for example Incomes Data Services Ltd, AIC/Inbucon Ltd, as well as the Department of Employment, provide information on current rates, trends in earnings and so forth. By whatever method, some idea of rates for key jobs needs to be established as a reference point from which to derive related levels of remuneration for other jobs in the hierarchy. There is nothing very precise about the methodology. No more than guidelines can be obtained. Scope therefore exists for modification and adaptation, which might be narrowed down by negotiation, still leaving considerable flexibility for a firm to influence the sort of wage/salary structure it wishes to see emerge.

Key jobs with known monetary values then become the cornerstones for the remaining part of the operation. These are the jobs which have been priced with regard to both external and internal considerations; it is fundamental that there be agreement about rates for key jobs. The rest of the process is administrative and judgemental. Key jobs fall within grades. The more key jobs, already priced, which fall within a particular grade the more reference points we have for moving to a position where we can decide the upper and lower limits of pay, the spread of range, for each grade. Once again, precision is lacking. This is one of the most unsatisfactory planks of the ranking technique. Had we wanted more precision here we would have opted for one of the quantitative techniques. According to the outcome of negotiation or company pay policy the spread of range must be decided in absolute terms. One needs to take a broad view and consider the total job hierarchy, the relationships between grades, rather than be too concerned with the niceties of arriving at any one individual grade's spread of range. Questions of overlap become important. The main function of overlap is to provide flexibility for rewarding people of merit or seniority of service who for one reason or another cannot yet be promoted to the next successive grade. A wide spread of range provides the same function within a grade. Both overlap and spread of range should increase as one moves up the hierarchy so that headroom for making personal adjustments increases among more senior jobs which tend to become more specialised. Another reason is that, rightly or wrongly, it has been general practice where free market conditions prevail, to make salary increases for individual performance on a percentage basis, resulting in higher absolute movements in the higher echelons. Diagrammatically the resultant grading and pricing structure is illustrated in Figure 4.3. The same five grades are employed as in Figure 4.2 and hypothetical indication is given of degrees of overlap and spread of range. For the sake of simplicity the scale extends only to a maximum of £4,000 but could be continued beyond.

It may well be in some areas of the organisation that the grades are too wide. Particularly the problem might present itself at the lower levels where a large number of jobs predominate. Clear differences between jobs do not show up in the ranking system. Maybe very little significant difference exists between in-grade jobs. On the other hand an organisation may wish to make marginal differences in compensation for marginal differences in work, or wish to have a tighter structure overall. In this case there is no reason why any existing grade should not further be subdivided into a number of subgrades according to function, job family, etc., with a separate subrange of rates within the parent grade band. What we are really saying is that the number of grades is wide open according to administrative, political and operational desiderata and that pay scales in practice are likely to be as much due to company policy as to job evaluation.

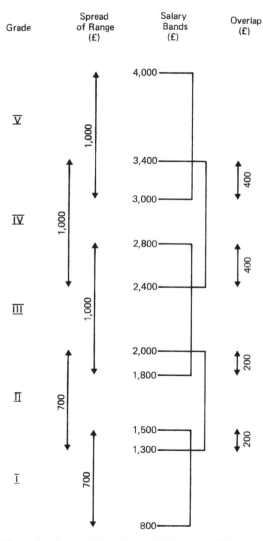

Fig. 4.3   Scale of Grades and Monetary Values

63

It is sometimes difficult to substantiate the reasons for particular decisions made in ranking since they are not formally recorded in writing as in some other schemes. Channels for consultation and redress must be provided. On the whole ranking is greeted with a high level of acceptability. Compared with more elaborate schemes of job evaluation, ranking is one of the easiest for employees to understand. The systems of ranking and pricing are straightforward procedures leading to an equitable rationalisation of a pay structure. At the end of the exercise no one should be grossly overpaid or underpaid. At least anomalies will have to be identified and presumably appropriate action taken. No one pretends that it is completely accurate or objective. The problems of the subjectivity of the assessors, their biases and degrees of familiarity with the work content of jobs are not unimportant. One should make the point, however, that they are prevalent to some extent in all job evaluation schemes. The main advantage of ranking is its simplicity. In business life it is sometimes better to arrive at a workable framework quickly than spend a long time hammering out a perfect solution.

CLASSIFICATION

The classification method (sometimes called 'predetermined gradings', or in American literature the 'grade description system') is basically a ranking operation in the sense that we end up with a structure of jobs marshalled into collective grades, but the procedure for achieving these is reversed. The idea germinated from work done in the Bureau of Personnel Research at the Carnegie Institute of Technology in 1922. The approach is more centralised, autocratic and closely related to organisational design. Initially, for an organisation, grades and their associated ranges of pay are predetermined. The job hierarchy is divided up into a number of grades, with written definitions developed for each grade, so that a fixed scale becomes the canon against which jobs are evaluated. Grade definitions take account of the differences in skill and responsibility between jobs on a very broad front. As in ranking, jobs are treated as 'wholes' and slotted into the structure, frequently on the basis of the pooled judgements of committees.

The logical starting point for setting up a classification system is to determine the shape and size of the organisational structure. For trading organisations and others which require a flexible, organic structure,

64

particularly in times of rapid economic, technological and social change, this initial constraint may impose too much rigidity. But for others which are more static, and particularly where public monies are concerned, a uniform system can be devised. Under the classification method, tighter control and budgeting can be exercised. Having defined the organisational structure, the next step is to establish a number of job grades, so that the organisation is divided up for administrative purposes into a series of occupational levels broadly distinguishable from each other in terms of their contributions and requirements. A

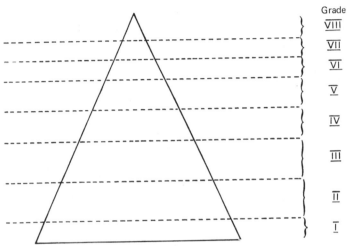

Fig. 4.4 Classification of an Organisation into Grades

diagrammatic illustration is given in Figure 4.4 where an organisational pyramid is subdivided for the sake of argument into eight grades, indicating differential stages in levels of responsibility. The horizontal grade demarcation lines are not drawn quite so arbitrarily as may appear at first sight from the diagram, but should in fact reflect the allocation of responsibilities as defined in a conventional organisation chart. For diagrammatic purposes we have assumed that each organisational level has been allocated to a grade definition. Roughly speaking this is the sort of picture we would expect to find in a classification system. In reality a number of closely allied organisational levels may in fact be grouped within the same grade.

Having determined the number of grades most appropriate to the organisation, which matter itself may well be the subject of joint

65

negotiation with trade unions or employee representatives, each grade should be defined quite clearly as to the level of responsibility and other demands one would expect to find within that grade. Grade definitions should then be recorded in writing. They form a formal yardstick against which other jobs may be evaluated, and slotted into the appropriate grade. Sometimes it is helpful to establish a bench mark job for each grade to facilitate the process of comparison. Criteria for the selection of bench mark jobs are exactly the same as discussed previously. It is then a relatively straightforward administrative procedure to classify all the jobs in an organisation according to the grade definitions. Once again, this should not be at the sole discretion of management, but the result of consensus reached in a properly constituted job evaluation committee.

The classification method is most commonly applied in branches of the public sector in the UK and elsewhere. One of the most notable examples is to be found in the United States Civil Service. 'Position classification' as it is called, originated from the 1949 Classification Act which established for the service a General Schedule of eighteen grades applying to most professional, administrative and technical jobs. Ranging from GS-1, covering simple, routine jobs through to GS-18, covering exceptionally demanding and difficult jobs, the scheme has stood the tests of time and acceptability, and provides for adequate discrimination between various levels of work. How many grades will be needed to produce a sufficiently discriminative and embracing framework is really a function of the size of an organisation and the range of activities in which it engages. As a general rule, the number of grades should be kept to a minimum so far as is compatible with the differentiation of responsibilities. The US Civil Service scheme is an exceptional example of the classification method applied to a large-scale organisation on a wide front. 'Generally speaking, jobs classified in GS-1 through GS-4 require less than a college education. Jobs in GS-5 through GS-11 are medium level technical, administrative and supervisory positions. Positions classified above GS-11 are distinctly high-level jobs, with compensation rates that reflect substantial differences between grades' (Patton, Littlefield, Self, 1964). Criticism has been levelled at the system, mainly on the grounds of the lack of objectivity in assessing a job before allocating it to a particular grade. Mistakes and misconceptions about a job at this point of the exercise can undermine the accuracy and consistency of the whole scheme. But as in any form of job evaluation, human judgement must be applied somewhere along the line, and carefully analysed and structured grade definitions, coupled with the pooled judgements of committees in allocating jobs to grades, should help to reduce inconsistencies to a minimum. No system is perfect, and such considerations did not prevent the Fulton Report on the UK Civil Service (1968) from recommending the adoption of the US type of classification scheme in Britain, where previously a multitude of grades and salary structures had tended to produce confusion and inflexibility. It is worth quoting from the evidence given to the Fulton Commission by the Institute of Personnel Management:

'The salary structures in the Civil Service appear unnecessarily numerous. It is difficult to believe that the number of separate departmental scales could not be drastically reduced and much more use made of common salary scales. Any movements in this direction would greatly facilitate the interchange of staff between departments. The length of salary scales, particularly at the lower levels, also seems excessive. The prospect of many years of slow predictable progression must have a considerable demoralising effect, particularly on the junior staff. Some scales could with advantage be reduced in length and consideration given to more flexible use of the incremental points to recognise individual ability and merit.'

The UK Civil Service had already operated a classification scheme, but it had become cumbersome, unwieldy and in many ways outmoded, for the nature of tasks, jobs and specialisms within the service had changed with the times, but the grading scheme had not. Fulton was the first fundamental investigation into the service for years, and its recommendations were made across a wide area, not simply confined to pay and grading, but including also matters of organisation, training and career development. Naturally a good deal of debate ensued, but despite some controversy, the recommendations in principle were accepted. On the pay side the government decided to abolish classes within the service and to undertake discussions with the civil service staff associations about introducing a unified grading structure covering all civil servants. The grading of each part was to be determined by job evaluation techniques. A salutory lesson can be drawn from this experience. Four years after the report of Fulton a unified system of common pay and grading had been introduced only at the top of the service, confined to the 700 or so top jobs of the rank of under-secretary and above which constitute the senior policy and management group. Below that level the National Whitley Council (1972) have consistently resisted the extension of unified grading because 'consensus cannot be reached' about the way job evaluation is to be implemented. The re-shape of the Civil Service is taking the form of abolishing classes and replacing them with new 'categories' and 'occupational groups' for pay, grading and other personnel management purposes, but an overall, unified grading system is still a long way off, for the simple reason that the staff associations are doggedly protecting their sectional interests. Job evaluation frequently means rationalising an existing structure. As has been stressed before, it can never be made to work without the consent of the work-people for whom it is intended.

Classification provides the opportunity for a planned organisation. Where the establishment strength for each grade can be prescribed, and with a given number of grades, two particular advantages obtain. The first concerns manpower budgeting. In the current situation manpower costs are known accurately, and more important, can be broken down to their respective levels. Where public monies are concerned this can act as a clear policy guide in matters of general pay increases and personnel mobility between grades. Moreover, costs in the future can be forecast with precision according to the various projected assumptions about organisational structure and establishments. Second, and as a corollary, well-defined career development pathways and progressions can be built in. It is far easier to hammer out not only promotion policy, but all aspects of personnel policy within a stable organisational framework than it is in the more tortuous, haphazard structures common to industrial and commercial life. Classification is very much the *forte* of the public sector. In Britain it is to be found in central and local government, in the armed services, the police force and the educational services, to mention the main areas. Indeed, it may well be that the total sum of money which can be voted to finance a service for a given period of time in the first place will determine the size, structure and internal relationships of an organisation.

However, it should not be assumed that classification is applicable only to the public sector. There are numerous examples to be found in private enterprise. The United States, which generally has a sophisticated and traditional attitude to job evaluation, favours its use widely. One of the most well known is that to be found in the US steel industry (Stieber, 1959) which is still in existence, and where the entire industry bases its pay for all levels of work on what is largely a classification system based on points ratings. The scheme originated from the intervention of the National War Labor Board, and today provides a measure of stability and rationality across the industry. No coercion exists; the scheme offers broad guidelines which individual firms may interpret according to local needs and conditions. In Britain, classification is the second most widely used of the conventional techniques. There is some evidence to suggest that in the private sector, as opposed to its more organisation-wide use in the public sector, it is predominantly used for the evaluation of lower level jobs in administrative and office employment. Some firms operate a number of schemes conjointly. International Computers, for example, operates points rating (for managerial, professional, technical and similar staff positions), whole job ranking (for senior management positions), and classification (for administrative, operating, clerical, typing and secretarial, office staff and ancillary staff). One very widely used scheme for clerical jobs (Clerical Job Grading Schedule, 1964) has been developed by the Institute of Administrative Management (formerly the Institute of Office Management). Known still as the IOM scheme, it attempts to classify most types of clerical work into six clearly defined grades, A–F, according to difficulty and complexity of work. Grade A includes the lowest level of tasks which require no previous clerical experience, through to Grade F tasks which 'necessitate exercising an extensive measure of responsibility and judgement or the application of a professional technique'. Details of the scheme may be readily obtained from the Institute, which also publishes from time to time a *Clerical Salaries Analysis* giving a breakdown of prevailing market rates by age, sex and geographical location for the various grades of clerical work, to which reference can be made by firms seeking information on rates and trends in salaries for clerical employment. One was published in 1974.

One should not lose sight of the fact that the purpose of job evaluation is to determine guidelines for arriving at absolute wage and salary levels. Classification is no exception. In the two instances quoted, in the US steel scheme and in the IOM scheme, the matter is relatively simple. Reference need only be made to rates of pay obtaining elsewhere for jobs in the same grade. An organisation is then able to set or negotiate its own rates accordingly. Where a firm operates its own classification scheme for the purpose of arriving at internal consistencies, then the procedure for pricing the structure is not quite so straightforward, but the principle of making external comparison is no different. As per normal practice, bench mark jobs should be established for each grade and reference made to prevailing market rates. This process is exactly the same as described under ranking. From the agreed rates for bench mark jobs, the spread of range for each grade and degrees of overlap between grades can be decided on the basis of salary policy or the outcome of negotiations. We would arrive at a priced grading structure. Whereas under ranking it would form the ultimate part of the exercise, under classification it in fact forms our starting point, for jobs are then assessed individually and slotted into the appropriate grade for which pay has already been determined.

On balance, a classification system probably has greater validity when it forms part of an industry-wide or national scheme. A wider number of reference points permits more thorough cross-checking, and differentials in actual pay for any given type and level of job are likely to be minimised. Since pay for comparable work is one of the major bones of contention, classification on a wide net should arrive at a more equitable and acceptable solution. A private in-company classification scheme can arrive at little more than internal convenience. The experience of Sweden is interesting here, according to a report of the Swedish Central Organisation of Salaried Employees (TCO) (1966), where central pay negotiations carried out at national level provide the guidelines within which, at local level, individual salaries are determined within individual concerns. Were it not for a system of job classification, the situation would be far too messy even to contemplate. Salary statistics forming the basis of negotiations at national level are derived from the data supplied by individual organisations. For such information to be meaningful there is clearly a need to classify employees according to the content and difficulties of the jobs they are doing. A classification system on a national scale is analogous to the contours on a map linking places of equal height. Jobs falling within the limits of a classification (or places within contour lines) have essential characteristics in common and can be regarded as similar to all intents and purposes, if not exactly equal in every respect. The more elaborate the classification system, the finer the discrimination which can be made between jobs (as would obtain with a smaller vertical interval on a contour map). Also, by using a system of this kind, it is possible to calculate meaningful relative salary levels for an entire enterprise or for certain defined categories of employees, to facilitate personnel allocation planning and to forecast salary costs under different assumptions as to the type of organisation chosen.

Taken generally, classification systems sometimes give the impression of being rather arbitrary. They are certainly inflexible in that they are not sensitive to changes in the nature and content of jobs. One remedy is to see that jobs are upgraded or downgraded, but this requires fairly close monitoring for which facilities may not exist, and which are not inherent in the scheme. Conversely, new jobs can be slotted into the structure with relative ease—perhaps too easily—for the specific details do not need to be itemised. It is a non-analytical technique. Each grade definition takes the form of an overall compass of job requirements, and in each case may be quite wide, so that the resultant scale may measure a range of jobs with a correspondingly wide range of skills. Classification is more elaborate than ranking. Ranking incorporates no measuring scale whatsoever, whereas in a vague way, by virtue of grade descriptions, classification does. Classification 'represents a link in the historical development of job evaluation between ranking and a points system' (Lanham, 1955).

Chapter 5

Applying Conventional Job Evaluation Techniques—Quantitative

Dissent is sometimes provoked by the use of non-quantitative methods. It can sometimes be more difficult to justify and uphold decisions based on purely qualitative criteria. Speed and administrative simplicity, although clearly advantageous, may not of themselves guarantee success. For these reasons, more accurate attempts can be made by use of what are known as the quantitative techniques.

POINTS RATING

In 1926, an American, Merrill R. Lott wrote a book entitled *Wage Scales and Job Evaluation* describing what is generally thought to be the first points system, as developed in his company, the Sperry Gyroscope Co. Inc. Since then the system has undergone a number of refinements, and exists today as the most extensively used method of job evaluation in Britain and America, and can take the form of a wide number of variations on the original theme. The technique is analytical: jobs are broken down into their component parts for the purpose of making comparisons between them. It is also quantitative: numerical values are assigned to each constituent element of a job and the total value of the job is reckoned to be the summation of the numerical values (points scores) assigned to each particular element or job factor. Whereas under the classification system we had in mind some fairly arbitrary grade definitions by which to rank jobs on an overall basis, under the points system we are obliged to define very carefully a range of predetermined criteria to act as a standard framework by which to compare each job in the survey. The criteria which we decide to use are derived from a consideration and determination of the most essential elements common to the whole range of jobs to be evaluated. Normally these criteria are known as job factors. This immediately raises a problem and places some limitation on the use of the scheme. Jobs differ widely in their content and in their demands at different levels in the hierarchy and between different functions. A universal points rating scheme which can be applied to a whole organisation successfully is likely to be elusive. Although some examples do exist, they tend to be cumbersome, since an unwieldy number of factors must be included in order to encompass the whole range of job characteristics to be encountered. One of the assets of the points system is that it enables fine discriminations to be made between jobs, but this advantage is negated if too many factors are used, resulting in a blurring of criterion definitions, and inevitably, a certain amount of co-variance between factors. Expediency normally calls for the discrete treatment of job families, such as manual, clerical, managerial, etc., with points plans tailor-made for each family. In other words, jobs differ and accordingly need to be assessed by different factors. Just as the relevance of the factors may vary, so too can the relative importance of any one factor, or any group of them, within a particular constellation of factors. Some form of weighting the more important factors must therefore be built into the scheme. Having established the structure, jobs can be scored or quantified on a comparative basis. Conceptually the idea bears similarity to Viteles's job psychograph (1932) which analysed the specific abilities necessary for success in a particular job and rated them on a five-point scale according to their contribution to the job as a whole. To some extent also it derives from Flanagan's (1954) 'critical incident' technique in which crucial aspects of job performance are isolated for criteria development, since job evaluation is concerned with identifying compensatable job factors.

Developing a new points plant is rather involved. A rushed or inadequately prepared procedure will only result in anomalies and grievances, and if the outcome does not bear the marks of accuracy and acceptability, the exercise will have been worthless. The main steps in the process can be itemised:

1. Establish a representative committee with responsibility for job evaluation on the lines which have already been discussed.

2. Analyse a significant sample of jobs and prepare job descriptions and specifications (or job information sheets).

73

3. Select and define those factors which are considered to be most critical in determining the relative degrees of difficulty and responsibility between jobs. Factor identification is most important. For emphasis, it is worth repeating the basic principle that a range of factors must be established which can be applied to the whole gamut of jobs under consideration, that too few factors will reduce the discriminatory powers of the technique, whilst too many will introduce problems of co-variance.

4. Weight the factors according to their relative importance, since factors are not identical in their contribution to job performance, and compensatory adjustment must be made. Most commonly this takes the form of dividing each factor into a number of *degrees* to represent the intensity with which each factor may be present in a job. The methodology for arriving at this is as follows:

    (*a*)   Determine a numerical range of points for each factor representing the distance between the maximum and minimum scores likely to obtain for any job within the sample.

    (*b*)   Sub-divide each factor into a number of degrees.

    (*c*)   Award a points value for each degree, so that the highest degree value is equal to the maximum possible score for that factor, and similarly, the lowest degree value is equal to the minimum possible score for that factor. A differential series of possible ranges then exists for each factor and its constituent degrees.

5. Test run a selected number of key jobs, awarding scores per factor, summing the scores, and comparing the results to see if the dispersion in the relative rating of jobs conforms with the existing differentiation between jobs, with the type of pattern one wishes to see emerge, or with the results obtained by some other method. One should also cross-check factor by factor to see that there are no obvious discrepancies and that a measure of reliability has been obtained in the ratings. If the results are way off beam, then something is wrong with one or more of the variables, either with the selection of factors, or their weightings, or score values, or in the choice of key jobs in the first instance. Having carefully considered these possible sources of bias and contamination, only an iterative approach is likely to resolve the issue. When the system produces acceptable and equitable results we may proceed. Although time-consuming, methodical and painstaking attention to the groundwork will pay dividends later on.

6. Evaluate all the jobs in the cluster or family, to arrive at a composite numerical value for each job.

7. Price the system (e.g. by reference to market rates for selected key jobs) and establish a grading structure with spread of range and overlap according to organisational and salary policy.

Let us now consider each of these steps in detail, beginning with step 3 (the preparatory work for steps 1 and 2 having been discussed in Chapter 3).

Factor identification is clearly related to the types of job under consideration. Rather than have a host of individual factors, it may sometimes be more convenient to collect them into broad groups. An early and very widely used points scheme was devised by Kress (1939) for the National Electrical Manufacturers Association in the USA, in which he studied jobs under eleven characteristics, grouped under the four generic headings of 'skill', 'effort', 'responsibility' and 'job conditions'. Each generic group consisted of a number of specific subfactors, thus:

Generic Factors	Specific Subfactors.
Skill	Education
	Experience
	Initiative and ingenuity
Effort	Physical demand
	Mental and/or visual demand
Responsibility	For equipment or process
	For materials or product
	For safety of others
	For work of others
Job Conditions	Working conditions
	Hazards

The scheme was applied to hourly paid jobs, but the principle by which factors are chosen are the same for any group of jobs, simply by reference to those characteristics which appear most commonly across the job family. In the NEMA scheme each characteristic was divided into five degrees and weighted according to its considered importance *vis-à-vis* other factors. Effectively, each characteristic was rated on a five-point scale according to its degree of importance and awarded a points score. The higher the complexity of the job, the higher the summation of points scores, which could then be translated into monetary equivalents. Numerous experiments have since been conducted, using variable numbers of factors, points ranges, and means for conversion into money wages.

To take an example, the British Institute of Management (1970) suggests the following factor complex:

Generic Factor	Specific Subfactors
Acquired skill and knowledge	Training and previous experience General reasoning ability Complexity of process Dexterity and motor accuracy
Responsibilities and mental requirements	Responsibility for material or equipment Effect on other operations Attention needed to orders Alertness to details Monotony
Physical requirements	Abnormal position Abnormal effort
Conditions of work	Disagreeableness Danger

We will have a look at a few more schemes in closer detail, but before doing so a few matters need clarification. The most important of these is deciding on the numerical value for each factor and subfactor, determining the number of degrees within a factor, and their own respective values. In determining the weighting of factors there is no prescribed formula or scientific method which can help us. The assumption is, of course, that the value of all factors combined constitutes 100 per cent of the total job. Frequently it is helpful, having defined the factors, to place them in rank order. Better still if this can be done on the basis of pooled judgements of a well-constituted and well-selected group of assessors forming the job evaluation committee. It is sometimes argued that several shots be made at the exercise, with a time interval between each, to allow the emotions to clear. Firstly some agreement must be reached, either on the basis of consensus or by averaging the rankings of the various members of the committee. Ranking factors indicates their relative importance, but does not give any indication of

76

their absolute values. All that can be said is that the most important factors will receive the lion's share, and vice versa, and that other factors will have their proportional score values determined by a considered opinion of what appears to be a fair discrimination between them. We are then in a situation of being able to say, for example:

Factor A	30%
Factor B	25%
Factor C	20%
Factor D	15%
Factor E	5%
Factor F	5%
Total	100%

Similarly, for subfactors constituting a generic factor:

Generic Factor A (30%) consists, say, of	Subfactor x	50%
	Subfactor y	30%
	Subfactor z	20%

Subfactors must be accorded a relative weight, and together must account for 100 per cent of the generic factor. A breakdown in this way indicates relative factor strengths, and the next step is to decide what actual values shall be used, or the potential points score that could be awarded to any particular factor. We could start at the end, so to speak, and decide upon a maximum possible points score for any job, say 500 points. The NEMA scheme had a maximum of 500 and one frequently finds subsequent schemes utilising this particular figure, but it really does not matter one jot what the total maximum points score shall be. We could equally well decide upon 1,000, or maybe only 100. In any case the total is going to be broken down on a percentage basis for each factor. The only thing to consider is that where a large number of factors are used it might be better to have a larger maximum number to give us more manoeuvrability and headroom within subfactors than would be the case if a smaller number were chosen.

Generic factors are broken down very broadly and accorded a percentage of the total. Subfactors are the ones against which rating is actually going to be made, and we need some guidelines to help us make accurate and consistent judgements. For this reason *degrees* are employed. Each subfactor must be broken down into a number of degrees, say five, with each degree representing progressive increments in the

77

demands of the job according to that subfactor. Let us look at an example:

Subfactor: Previous Training (Occupational Group: Clerical Jobs)

1st degree   No specific training or experience required.

2nd degree   Some familiarity with office procedures required—particularly filing and copy-typing.

3rd degree   Proficiency in shorthand (100 wpm) and typing (60 wpm).

4th degree   Proficiency in shorthand (130 wpm) and typing (60 wpm) and reasonable degree of numeracy and literacy (e.g. CSE).

5th degree   Ability to initiate action through established clerical procedures; answer telephone enquiries and reply to letters without supervision; some supervision of junior clerical procedures. Normally GCE 'O' level.

Breaking a subfactor down into degree is always somewhat arbitrary. Some guidance can be obtained from the way work is actually organised within a department or group of departments. Some subfactors may be easier to quantify, for example 'experience':

Subfactor: Experience

1st degree   Up to 3 months
2nd degree   3 months—1 year
3rd degree   1—3 years
4th degree   3—5 years
5th degree   Over 5 years

Degrees are simply indications of the amount by which a subfactor may be present in a given job. Using 5 degrees to form a 5-point scale is largely a matter of administrative convenience. Any number of degrees could be used. One does not need a uniform number of degrees for different factors, some may require 6 or 7 degrees, others only 4.

Degrees having been established we are then in a position to assign numerical values to each particular degree. The maximum points available for the highest degree represents the maximum points score for that particular subfactor and vice versa.

The actual values ascribed to degrees may be determined by arithmetic or geometric progression, or by variable percentage differentials.

Arithmetic progression is the most common, and to illustrate this it would be useful to return again to the NEMA scheme:

		Degrees					
Generic Factor	Subfactors	1st	2nd	3rd	4th	5th	
Skill	Education	15	30	45	60	75	⎫
	Experience	20	40	60	80	100	⎬ Points
	Initiative and ingenuity	15	30	45	60	75	⎭

Arithmetic progression is in fact increasing the degree value by 100 per cent each time; the numerical difference between the degree is constant. Geometric progression, however, increases the degree values by 100 per cent of the *preceeding degree value* each time; the point value is doubled at each successive stage, and would obtain as follows:

	Degrees					
Subfactors	1st	2nd	3rd	4th	5th	
x	25	50	100	200	400	⎫
y	15	30	60	120	240	⎬ Points
z	10	20	40	80	160	⎭

Geometric progression clearly results in a wider points range, and thus may well be too wide for administrative purposes. A variable percentage progression could be used either to produce a narrower points range, or to overcome the fallacy built into both arithmetic and geometric progression, that degree values do in fact increase by a constant percentage each time. If a variable percentage scale were used, the percentage differential would normally increase as one moved up the degree range. Unfortunately, this could produce arbitrary and probably unwanted loadings in the higher degree range. It also makes the scheme more administratively complicated than it need be and produces a result which is probably less defensible.

To recap on the main issues so far: there are no hard and fast rules for ensuring that the right number of degrees are arrived at and that appropriate gradation exists between them. Largely it is a matter of experience and common sense, but as a general guideline it is useful to consider the range of jobs to which the system is to be applied from the point of view of the criterion variables which are likely to result in successful performance. So that, in deciding the number of degrees to be allocated to the factor of 'education', one should determine and specify the minimum amount of that factor likely to be called for in a given range of jobs. That level of education then assumes the degree of 1. Similarly, one then looks at the maximum amount of the education factor which is likely to be called for in that range, and if one is employing a 5-point scale, it assumes the degree of 5. The number of degrees must be wide enough to create a meaningful dispersion, but there is a danger of allocating too many degrees. Too few, however, will cramp the system by inhibiting its powers of discrimination. It is all too easy for 'central tendency' to creep into any rating scale, and careful and precise definition of degree characteristics should avoid this particular pitfall. The final outcome of the exercise of course must produce a ranking of jobs which is both logical and acceptable. A certain amount of trial and error with respect to weightings, degrees, etc., might have to be undertaken in order to produce the best result. In a way, one can make the system produce what one wants. To some extent the system is tautological, and this is cited as one of its major invalidities. Further attention will be given to this aspect in Chapter 7. The choice of factors, degrees and weightings is wide open. 'No one particular method appears to be so outstanding that all points plans utilise it. Here, as in other steps in the installation of job evaluation, a company needs to analyse and experiment with various methods in order that it may select the one which seems to solve its particular problems best' (Lanham, 1955).

Any scheme must be tailor-made to the requirements of the individual organisation. Questions of factor points allocations and degree weightings and so on are therefore highly variable affairs. Two examples have been selected and are included as appendixes. Appendix I reproduces a factor points scheme developed by the remuneration planning department of International Computers Ltd (1969) for managerial staff and incorporates as its main factors: mental requirements; training, experience and maturity; communications; creative requirements; discretionary responsibility; accountability; and personnel responsibilities. This is an elaborate scheme with guidance in its instructions for rating each factor and allowing fairly broad interpretation of points scores within factors. A further example of a factor points rating scheme, this time based initially on the direct consensus method developed by Associated Industrial Consultants Ltd for the senior salary structure of the Post Office, is tabled as Appendix II. Both schemes cover a wide, comprehensive factor range and give clear explanations to raters. The quasi-confidential nature of these schemes precludes a detailed comparative analysis.

Strictly speaking, points systems may be classified as 'simple points systems' in which factors are not subdivided into degrees, but in which a straightforward points range is allocated to each factor (for example, 0–50; or if it is felt there is a minimum level which requires compensation, 10–50) as opposed to a 'weighted points system' with appropriate degrees and scores. The administrative simplicity of the one system must be considered against the greater accuracy of the other. Frequently one finds hybrid examples of schemes in which there is a certain amount of weighting without going into the elaboration of defining exact degrees. The 20-factor scheme developed by the Trades Union Congress for a wide range of weekly paid staff employs a weighted points range for each factor without a full complement of specific degree values, thus allowing a measure of freedom and flexibility in the scoring. An extract is shown in Appendix III. A further actual example will add clarification. In 1966 the London Boroughs' Management Services Unit embarked on a job evaluation programme of 42,000 clerical, administrative, professional and technical posts in 27 of the 32 London boroughs and including a small number of posts in the Greater London Council with the consent and co-operation of the Greater London Whitley Council, the joint negotiating body, and the National Association of Local Government Officers and the National Union of Public Employees, the two main unions. Nine generic factors were employed with varying numbers of subfactors and points ranges (Thomson, 1968). An extract is shown in Appendix IV.

Another way of acknowledging that jobs have a minimum level of demand which may not show up in the allocation of factor weightings and degree values, and recognising also that the totality of a job is greater than the sum of its individual parts, is by the use of a *datum*. A datum is a flat-rate addition (e.g. 100 points) to the total points score of each job. The thing to watch for is that the datum does not constitute too large a proportion of the total points score, or it will neutralise the differentials obtained from the exercise. Although the absolute value of the datum is constant, its relative value will vary from job to job; it will have a larger value in those jobs which come out with a low points score, and conversely, a smaller value in those jobs with a high points score. It is difficult to say what an ideal datum value should be. It will not have contributed much if it constitutes only 10 per cent of the total score, and if it constitutes more than 25 per cent we are getting to the point where it negates the purpose of the exercise. The preference of many job evaluators is to ignore the datum altogether. Its inclusion at an arbitrary flat-rate tends to skew distribution. The fact that it should sometimes be felt necessary is a sad reflection on the reliability and validity of the points system devised. On the other hand schemes are often more acceptable to the people whose jobs are being evaluated if a datum is in fact included. In that case, it may be better to add to the points scores a datum which increases logarithmically.

A points rating system is only a preliminary to arriving at an equitable pay structure. 'Unfortunately, there are no scientific principles to guide us in this process. The question of how much money should be paid cannot be deduced in a completely objective fashion. Such problems as labour shortage, union pressure, market rates, company profitability and employee attitudes all affect the answer in varying proportions from time to time' (BIM, 1970). However, we can arrive at a closer and more accurate relationship between money and job worth by the point system than by any other conventional method. To begin with, we have composite quantitative values for all jobs, each job having been scored and the points scores summated. The summation for each job as a whole indicates its relative position in the hierarchy and, more precisely, the numerical relationship between one job and another. These results are shown in Table 5.1.

The task now is to convert points scores into monetary values. It should be emphasised that by no means does the numerical relationship between jobs indicate precise differentiations in monetary value between them. For one reason, the scoring is never perfectly accurate, and for another, as we have said before, many factors other than value of jobs need to be taken into account in determining the pay for an individual and in the determination of a pay policy as a whole. Points scores are no more than a guide to the relative dispersion of jobs.

As a first step one needs some frame of reference in monetary terms against which to relate individual points scores. Common practice is to plot a graph with points ratings on the x axis and money on the y axis. For points ratings a standard measuring yardstick has already been established, but this is not so of course in the case of a pay scale, which is what we are trying to ascertain, and in order to achieve this we must for a moment ignore conventional mathematical orthodoxy. There are a number of alternatives open to an organisation. One is to plot points scores against current wage or salary rates already obtaining, a tactic which is possible where job evaluation is being superimposed on to an

Table 5.1

Job Type	Points Score
A	180
B	183
C	188
D	190
E	195
F	205
G	214
H	222
I	238
J	270
K	275
L	290
M	315
N	350
O	375
P	410
Q	500
R	580
S	675
T	760
U	840
V	850
W	950
X	1050

existing pay structure. A scattergram indicating the relationship between job evaluation scores and rates of pay can then be plotted, as in Figure 5.1, and will normally show a positive correlation, provided the original rates of pay or the points scores are on the whole not too much out of alignment. This tautological procedure might astound the reader, but it does have the merit of revealing those jobs which may be grossly out of alignment in terms of overpayment or underpayment. It might equally reveal fallacies in the points scoring. In any event, jobs which do not conform to the general trend should be the subject of closer scrutiny and re-evaluation. In Figure 5.1 an anomalous job is

83

indicated at position A. Having plotted all the points a best-fitting line (mean) can be drawn in by visual inspection, ensuring that roughly the same number of points falls below as above the line. Figure 5.2 illustrates such a trend line drawn through a scatter of points. More accurately it can be determined by the statistical technique of 'least squares', or similar statistical procedures to find the best-fitting parabola if visual examination suggests that the points would be more faithfully represented by such a curve. Drawing the pay curve by eye might be

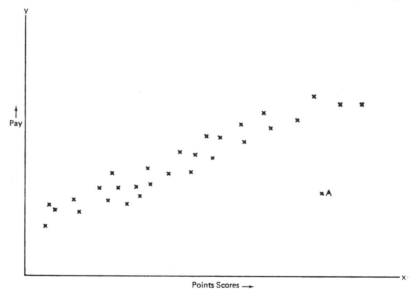

Fig. 5.1   Scattergram of Job Evaluation Scores

just as reliable in the long run, as well as simpler where very little dispersion occurs, since rates of pay and ranges of points scores are later going to be averaged out into grade boxes anyway. An alternative method an organisation might choose to adopt, and indeed will be obliged to if no current pay rates exist as might happen under conditions of expansion, is to select a number of key jobs or bench mark jobs at various points throughout the range, determine their market rate, plot points against pay on a similar graph, and use them as anchorages or references in the determination of pay for other jobs in the survey whose points scores are known and for which it is desired to produce an equitable rate *vis-à-vis* bench mark jobs. Yet a third alternative, and one which occurs in practice much more than textbooks would lead one to suppose, is for the organisation to plot the points on the abscissa as before, and to draw the pay curve it would like to see in the form of a progressive pay structure as part of its policy for career development on the ordinate later. The slope of the curve, by whatever method, is in the last resort nearly always the subject of negotiation or company policy. Salary administrators, and wage negotiators too for that matter, are concerned to see that the average rate of increase in the slope of the pay

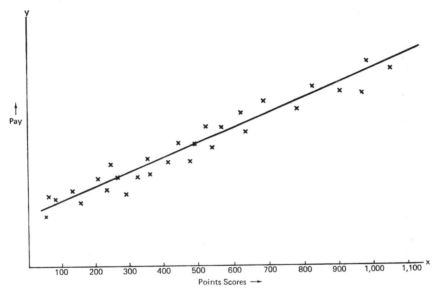

Fig. 5.2   Trend Line through a Scatter of Points

curve—i.e. the average rate at which pay increases as jobs increase in evaluated points—fits in and forms part of a comprehensive strategy for organisational effectiveness, in so far as job grades, formal structure and opportunities for individual progression are concerned. Apart from movements along the curve, an organisation might wish to push the whole schedule itself upwards or downwards according to pay policy. The graph is just a work-sheet on which to experiment and come to decisions about pay.

As in the previously explained techniques of job evaluation, some form of grading structure is necessary in which to marshal jobs of comparable responsibility and at comparable levels in the organisation, if

85

only to reduce the mass to manageable proportions. Jobs are not simply paid-off *pro rata* against points scores. Grades also have other functions, and must be established according to well thought-out criteria, such as the organisation structure which seems most appropriate for purposes of planning and control, in order to obtain compatibility with an existing organisational structure, to fit a sequential series of levels in the hierarchy in the light of career development policy, to provide a linear or exponential progression in an individual's projected earnings over time, to fit market rates, or to fit or form the basis of salary policy generally.

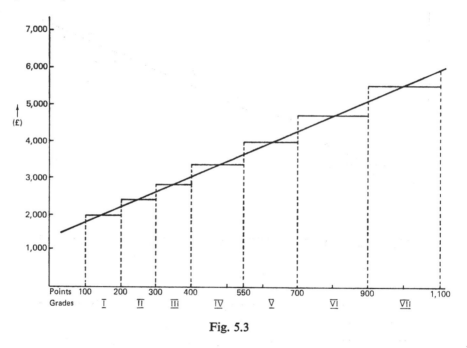

Fig. 5.3

The number of grades an organisation will need will depend on its size and the variation in the levels of jobs involved. Small organisations may need no more than four or five grades, whilst larger ones may need as many as a dozen or so in order to cope adequately and fairly. Various policy considerations in determining grade demarcation lines have been mentioned, but sometimes one finds natural breaks occurring in the sequence, reflecting differences in responsibility and organisational importance, and where they occur such breaks should be utilised. As in ranking and classification techniques, we must consider grade demarcation lines, the spread of range within grades, the degree of overlap between grades and the definition of grade boxes with adequate headroom for the reward of individual performance, merit, length of service and so on.

Using the points information and trend line adopted in the previous examples, Figure 5.3 employs dotted vertical lines to indicate grade demarcation lines coinciding with the 100, 200, 300, 400, 550, 700, 900 and 1,100 point intervals. The model to be based on these data is hypothetical, but has been constructed to reveal the main issues involved. Preliminary observations to be made are that a wide points range has been used to avoid bunching. Also it should be assumed that the scheme has been devised for a wide range of staff jobs, and the structure has been priced. The spread of points range per grade increases as one moves up the hierarchy. This is because jobs differentiate more in the higher echelons and questions of personal worth of incumbents become more pertinent. Also it becomes more difficult to measure the precise contribution of a job in comparison to its organisational neighbours. Horizontal lines have been drawn through the mid-points of the trend line for each grade. This line represents the median salary for jobs falling within its respective points range.

Having determined the median according to the rates which currently obtain, the next decision to be made is what spread of range in salary should apply for each grade in order to provide adequate headroom. A consistent policy needs to be followed throughout. A company might decide to apply a uniform degree in spread of range across the board, or possibly to increase it slightly towards the top. In the figures we are referring to, in Grade I (points range 100–200) a median salary of £1,900 obtains. In determining the spread of range we are seeking to establish a ceiling and a floor, a maximum and minimum range of pay within which to pay people within that grade. The variance in pay from the median to provide maximal and minimal limits must in absolute terms be the same in both directions, upwards and downwards, or else by definition £1,900 will cease to be the median. True, a company may decide that what comes out as the median may be too high or too low to start with, and adjust it accordingly. Assuming no such problem arises, and that median levels are acceptable, the simplest and most expedient way is to decide upon what percentage of the median figure itself would provide a spread of range in which to accommodate most of the jobs within the grade and provide adequate headroom. In the example presented, a spread of range of 40 per cent of the median has been adopted in Grades I to VI, and in Grade VII it has been increased to 50 per cent for the most senior jobs in the sample, where one would expect to find a higher degree of individual variation and where a little more headroom is useful to compensate for increases in marginal taxation. To return to Grade I, a spread of range of 40 per cent provides a variance of ±£380, giving a minimum salary of £1,520 and a maximum of £2,280. In Grade II, a spread of range of 40 per cent provides minimal and maximal salaries of £1,880 and £2,820 against a median of £2,350. Similarly through to Grade VII, where a spread of range of 50 per cent, not uncommon at higher levels but rarely exceeded, provides minimal and maximal salaries of £4,125 and £6,875 against a median of £5,500. These details are given in Table 5.2 below.

Table 5.2

Points Range	Grade	Median (£)	Percentage Spread of Range (%)	Variance from Median	Actual Spread of Range (£)	Minimum Salary (£)	Maximum Salary (£)
100–200	I	1,900	40	±380	760	1,520	2,280
201–300	II	2,350	40	±470	940	1,880	2,820
301–400	III	2,800	40	±560	1,120	2,240	3,360
401–550	IV	3,400	40	±680	1,360	2,720	4,080
551–700	V	4,000	40	±800	1,600	3,200	4,800
701–900	VI	4,750	40	±950	1,900	3,800	5,700
901–1,100	VII	5,500	50	±1,375	2,750	4,125	6,875

Having established the spread of range for each grade, we can superimpose this information on to our graph or work-sheet, as shown in Figure 5.4, connecting up appropriate points ranges with salary ranges to form grade boxes. Grade boxes indicate the areas, increasing in size as one moves up the scale, within which an organisation has freedom to monœuvre its rates of pay and still be consistent with salary policy. It should be clear that we are by no means attempting to let a fixed allocation of points equal a fixed allocation of money. The outcome is far more flexible. Many of the discrepancies and errors of judgement which might have crept into the rating procedure, or likewise into the determination of pay levels in relation to points scored, are ironed out in the formation of fairly broad grade boxes. Removing the trend line and medians from our diagram, which now for the purposes of salary administration have become redundant, we are left with a straightforward, but carefully arrived at, grading structure as in Figure 5.5.

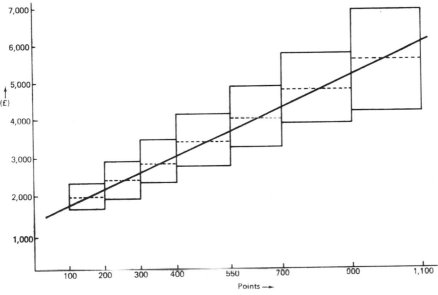

Fig. 5.4

It will be noted that a progressive increase in the degree of overlap between grades has also been achieved, normally reckoned to be a plus factor in times of organisational change, where the content of jobs may not be static over long periods and where they can be re-evaluated without deleteriously affecting the personal incomes of the job holders in the short run. As has been mentioned before, it also provides a high degree of scope for merit rating and length of service, and it is possible in theory for a job holder in a given grade to receive a rate of remuneration in excess of certain members of the next successive grade. In the model we have constructed, a narrow band of overlap in salary range is common to these grades. For example, a salary level of £3,300 occurs at varying intervals within grades III, IV and V. This is one way by which anomalies may easily be overcome. Flexibility has its advantages, but it also has its price. There is plenty of room for confusion and internal politics with expansive, overlapping grades. Organisations seeking a tighter, more rigid structure would find it appropriate, and a relatively simple matter, to create a number of subgrades within any one individual grade, or alternatively, to restructure the whole exercise by employing a larger number of grades overall.

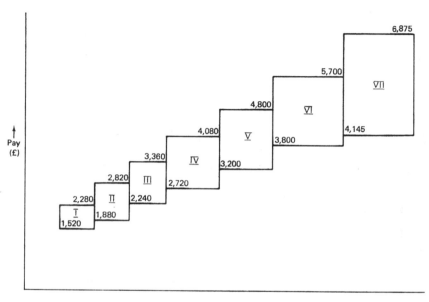

Fig. 5.5

FACTOR COMPARISON

Factor comparison is a technique which embodies the principles of points rating with the principle of ranking. It is analytical in that jobs are broken down into factors. Fewer factors are usually used than in a points system proper, for speed and simplicity, but the method can become complicated in its application, arising from the need to reconcile two independent sets of ratings. The first set of ratings consists of the rank order of jobs under various factor headings. The second set consists of monetary values ascribed to each constituent factor of a job so that the money value of any factor is in alignment with its predetermined rank order. Although this may sound relatively straightforward, it can in practice give rise to major headaches. The assignment of factor rankings in an ordinal series gives no clues as to the relative

90

differences between them for the purposes of pricing, which are, after all, the crucial decision to be made. The outcome is therefore bound to remain rather arbitrary or deliberately geared to fit the existing system. Experience shows that this is the technique which employees generally have most difficulty in understanding, and together with its rather messy and time-consuming *modus operandi*, probably accounts for the fact that it is the least used of the conventional systems in British organisations.

The origins of factor comparison are attributed to Eugene Benge (Benge, Burk and Hay, 1941) who worked in America, and experimented with and modified some of the earlier systems of Mitten, Lott, Kress and others. In the Benge study, jobs are subdivided into five generic compensable factors, namely: mental requirements, skill requirements, physical requirements, responsibility, working conditions. To administer the scheme the initial task is to define the factors most relevant to the jobs in question. Although Benge selected five factors in a schedule originally devised for hourly paid jobs, there is no reason why five should be the most appropriate number in each case, nor do they have to be as specified. If the scheme is to be used for junior clerical staff, for example, a different factor complex might be more desirable. One well-used variation of the scheme in the USA substitutes 'supervision' for 'working conditions'. In general, mental requirements, responsibilities and skill requirements are likely to be the key factors, but others may suggest themselves as common and fundamental from a careful study of the job descriptions and specifications. The whole idea of the scheme is to identify just a few, broad factors, probably at least four and no more than seven.

The next step is to select a number of bench mark jobs. This is always a crunch point in job evaluation, but under the factor comparison scheme becomes even more critical, for the final evaluation of other jobs is made against the fixed rate of payment obtaining for bench mark jobs. This fixed rate may be the current rate prevailing, or the rate which the organisation intends to pay, having conducted a wage or salary survey to get an idea of the market level, or the rates resulting from joint negotiation. In any event, the prevailing or intended rate for a bench mark job must be agreed. It must propose to carry what is generally regarded as the correct payment. There must be no dispute about it. A bench mark job must also be clearly divisible into generic factors. It should almost go without saying by now that the pooled judgements of a properly constituted job evaluation committee are called for. Assessors must agree the determination of bench mark jobs, and even more important, must also be in agreement about the relative value which each factor plays within that bench mark job when it is successfully executed. First the constituent factors must be given relative positions according to their individual contribution to the total (this is sometimes done on a percentage basis), and following from that, the total sum of money obtaining for a bench mark job can be broken down and awarded in absolute terms to each factor. This is an exceedingly tricky exercise, and highly subjective. It is this process, both in the preliminary bench mark analyses, and in the final sweep, that gives rise to greatest contention and controversy. Moreover, bench mark jobs must possess all the qualities one would normally expect to find. They must bear strong family relationship with the other jobs to be evaluated, and should be sufficiently representative of all current levels of pay and seniority within the group.

So far we have outlined the basic considerations, namely that factor comparison involves two distinct stages: (a) factor ranking, and (b) factor evaluation. As the name implies, jobs are to be evaluated comparatively, factor by factor. The essential difference between factor comparison and points rating, the other analytical technique, is that here no independent scale or yardstick is used. Jobs are compared against each other. Factor ranking means that, beginning with bench mark jobs, the constituent factors must be placed in rank order according to their relative importance or contribution to the job as a whole.

To take an example, let us assume we are faced with a payment problem for a group of employees in an office services department of a fairly typical commercial head office. We might expect to find a number of people, depending on the size of the organisation, fulfilling the following roles: cleaner, porter, receptionist, telephonist, storeman, tea lady, chauffeur, garage hand, office services supervisor, assistant i/c stationery, assistant i/c photocopying and duplicating. Bench mark jobs are selected according to the criteria discussed. In this case the cleaner and the receptionist emerge, for the sake of argument, as the most suitable bench mark jobs. Both have role specifications which are clearly understood, and there is no disagreement about the wage rates which apply. The receptionist is paid £30 per week and the cleaner £15 per week.

Using the Benge factor complex, the committee decides the relative importance of each factor in each job. Factor rankings can then be tabulated as in Table 5.3.

Table 5.3

Factor Rankings of two Bench Mark Jobs

Factor Rank Order	*Cleaner*	*Receptionist*
1	Physical requirements	Skill requirements
2	Working conditions	Responsibility
3	Skill reqts	Mental reqts
4	Responsibility	Physical reqts
5	Mental reqts	Working conditions

To get a clearer picture of the interrelationships between the two jobs, we must integrate both of them by rank order under the generic factor headings, as in the matrix in Table 5.4.

Table 5.4

Matrix of Factor Rankings

Rank Order	*Mental Reqt.*	*Skill Reqt.*	*Physical Reqt.*	*Responsibility*	*Working Conditions*
1		Receptionist	Cleaner		
2				Receptionist	Cleaner
3	Receptionist	Cleaner			
4				Receptionist	Cleaner
5	Cleaner				Receptionist

This part of the exercise is not just an administrative nicety, but an essential step to which we will have to refer again later. Meanwhile, it should be noted that the matrix is something like a map, and shows up the relative differences between the two jobs at a glance. It does not indicate absolute differences, which is what we are aiming at, and which must be determined by the process of factor evaluation.

Factor evaluation is the name given to that part of the exercise which ascribes monetary values to each factor. If the composite wage is known, then each factor must have a certain value. The sum total of the factor values constitute 100 per cent of the composite wage. For each of the two bench mark jobs, then, we must decide what each factor is

93

worth. Our example, for purposes of clarity, is highly simplistic. The results of our deliberations can be shown as in Table 5.5.

Table 5.5

Factor Evaluation of two Bench Mark Jobs

	Receptionist (£)	Cleaner (£)
Mental	6	1
Skill	10	3
Physical	4	5
Responsibility	8	2
Working conditions	2	4
	£30	£15

The next step is to reconcile the results obtained from factor evaluation with those obtained from the original ranking of factors. In other words, there must be conformity between the relative differences indicated by ranking and the absolute differences we have arrived at by our rather arbitrary and subjective monetary allocations. In practice this does not always work out quite so easily. The easiest way to cross-check is to return to our matrix, and add in the monetary values, as shown in Table 5.6.

Table 5.6

Matrix of Factor Rankings and Factor Evaluations

Rank Order	Mental Reqts	Skill Reqts	Physical Reqts	Responsibility	Working Conditions
1		Receptionist (£10)	Cleaner £(5)		
2				Receptionist (£8)	Cleaner (£4)
3	Receptionist (£6)	Cleaner (£3)			
4			Receptionist (£4)	Cleaner (£2)	
5	Cleaner (£1)				Receptionist (£2)

In our example, no contradictions arise. For example, under 'mental requirements', the receptionist is ranked higher than the cleaner, and the factor wage values are £6 and £1 respectively. Similarly, for skill,

94

the actual cash values are in accordance with factor rankings. No glaring anomalies exist. Were they to do so, both processes of factor ranking and factor evaluation would have to be thought out anew, and the results 'juggled' until both sets of results become consistent. The technique is of course far less accurate than points rating, but it is likely to be more reliable than the whole job ranking techniques because we are comparing jobs against each other from two points of view which are complementary, rather than from one overall point of view. It must be admitted that none of it is very scientific, but the main advantage is that we are able to pinpoint the precise areas of a job which may give rise to disagreement. As has been said before, it is on the whole more important to arrive at a solution which is acceptable and workable than one which contains scientific purity. Even in our simple example, ground for quibble may arise under the factor of 'physical requirements', where despite a wide differentiation in factor rank order between the two jobs, the difference is reflected in actual cash terms by an amount of only £1. This would most likely be the subject of debate, and some adjustment made.

Our example has been reduced to fundamentals. In a real-life situation, with far more jobs to evaluate, as many as a dozen or so bench mark jobs may be needed. Other jobs in the group are then compared against the bench mark jobs, first factor by factor to determine their rank order, and then their factor values are assessed in cash terms. The sum of factor values equals the total pay for each job. As before, the twin processes of factor ranking and factor evaluation must be compared and reconciled. Jobs are evaluated against each other by comparing them with a rating scale related to the current monetary values actually being paid. The initial stage, the pilot run with the bench mark jobs, is the hardest part. Once some structure emerges, the business of ranking and evaluating becomes easier since there are more reference points against which to make comparison. All the time it must be remembered that it is the job and not the incumbent which is to be rated. It is particularly important that assessors be thoroughly familiar with all the jobs, especially bench marks. Lack of familiarity can only result in errors and confusion. It is sometimes argued that the exercise be repeated several times, with a period of a week or two between each operation, to check for reliability in the ratings. A common cause of lack of consistency can be attributed to 'halo' effects. Factors, of course, are not necessarily of equal importance, and one should beware of generalising for the job as a whole from the evaluation of one or two factors. It should not be assumed that jobs rank high or low in all factors. As we have seen, the relative position of jobs can vary quite widely under various factors.

Overall, factor comparison is more appropriately applied to hourly paid and other less complex jobs in general. It can be adapted for white-collar employment, but in the UK tends not to be, although one does find occasional examples of it in the traditional so-called black-coated areas of junior clerical and office jobs. Usage in the US is more wide-spread, where the technique has made considerable inroads in the fields of insurance and banking.

Factor comparison has engendered perhaps rather more criticism than the other conventional techniques. The operational difficulties are already apparent. Apart from the logistics, the technique is liable to considerable contamination from error variance and rating bias. Moreover, the criterion of present wage structure for a key job could be regarded as the most unholy crime of all. It is clearly the worst potential source of invalidity. One must have some sort of starting point, and the only precautions one can take are to ensure absolute agreement about the choice of a bench mark job, about the market rate prevailing within the locality or in the industry according to the normal frame of reference obtaining for a particular organisation, about the pay policy to be adopted, and about the differential values of constituent factors. Subjectivity and consensus lie at its very root. As regards the reliability of ratings, in the original Benge study, ratings made by the assessors were repeated on three separate occasions with an interval of one week between each, and produced, it is reported (Benge, Burke and Hay, 1941), a high correlation between ratings. In some ways this is made easier by concentrating on just a few factors. The risk of double-counting that may arise from co-variance between factors, as in a points system, is avoided. Deriving from the selection of factors and bench mark jobs, factor comparison lends itself exclusively to the treatment of job families. It cannot be used on a wide ambit to encompass a whole range of dissimilar and hierarchically dispersed jobs. To do so would involve the determination of a whole series of independent schemes aimed at specific areas, and as a corollary, thus applied to large organisations, would result in a series of disconnected structures. If the

96

objective of job evaluation is to achieve conformity and comparability across the board, factor comparison, lacking generality, would be unsuitable. It is therefore more relevant to smaller companies or smaller groups of jobs, where a points system may not be feasible, but where on the other hand it is likely to be more accurate than job ranking.

Chapter 6

Some Developments in Job Evaluation Techniques

TIME-SPAN OF DISCRETION THEORY

One of the more interesting and controversial theories for the determination of payment is that developed in recent years by Professor Elliott Jaques now of Brunel University, arising out of a more comprehensive investigation into organisational structure, roles and relationships at the Glacier Metal Company, a light engineering company to the west of London. His findings form part of what is generally known as the Glacier Project. Reference was made to the genesis of his ideas in a discussion of the socio-psychological aspects of pay in Chapter 2. Now we must look more closely at the application of the theory to the problem of determining differentials. The totality of Jaques's postulates forms an integrated behavioural theory. It is not difficult to disentangle the main threads of thought, but it is sometimes difficult to know where to start.

Jaques tackles the problem of equitable payment from a number of angles. He seeks, first, a means to determine the appropriate payment and status for individuals for the work they do, so that each one has a sense of fair and just return for their work; and second, to determine a pattern of payment that is economically sound. He argues that there is a clear and unequivocal scale for expressing payment, namely in monetary terms, but that no such equivalent and unequivocal scale exists for measuring individual capacities or levels of work. In the absence of tangible measuring yardsticks, assessments about the things for which money is paid are made on the basis of subjective judgements and assumptions. He criticises job evaluation on these grounds, and claims that conventional methods of determining wages and salaries rest on the relative strengths of the parties engaged in negotiation or bargaining. Jaques sees an endemic and destructive source of conflict here; the laws which govern wage-fixing are the laws of the jungle. The most powerful groups survive, as in a sort of social Darwinism, and exert power over the less powerful groups. The fundamental, metaphysical conception is that of homeostatis. In a system free from constraints, there is a natural, self-equilibrating order in things. Job evaluation, in his view, perpetuates the felony of artificial adjustments to employment problems and produces skewed distributions of social and economic satisfactions. He proposes a system which is 'scientific' and 'objective', eschewing political power and negotiation. The solution to the problem of inequitable distribution of wealth can only be arrived at by the correct interpretation of social reality [*sic*] which leads to the 'requisite policy' or that policy demanded by the nature of things.

One of the recurring themes in his writings is his reference to the conceptual trilogy of 'work-payment-capacity', abbreviated W, P, C. The assertion is that we each have an unconscious awareness of the level of work of which we are capable, of the level of work we are doing in our current role, and of the equitable payment levels for both the level of work we are in fact doing and the level of work we feel capable of doing. So that an individual can be in a state of equilibrium, a situation must exist where the demands of the job are consistent with personal capacity for doing it (C = W) and the rate of payment received must be regarded as fair and equitable. Jaques represents the equilibrium position as C-W-P. By permutation, thirteen different alignments of these variables are possible. For illustration:

C-W-P   capacity matches work of correct payment, a state of equilibrium; or

C-W
| where job demands are in accordance with capacity but payment is below par, a situation likely to give rise to feelings of inequitable treatment; or
P

C-P
| where an individual's capacity exceeds the work demands made upon him but where payment is consistent with capacity, a situation likely to give rise to feelings of frustration; or
W

P
|
W
|
C

where payment is too high for the level of work, and where the level of work is above individual capacity, a strong stress-inducing situation; and so on.

Disequilibrium in the W-P-C relationship is a maladjustment giving rise to feelings of stress, guilt, inequity, frustration or other 'neurotic disjunctions between an individual's capacity and his work' (Jaques, 1970). The ideal of matching individual ability to work is not new. Personnel managers and industrial psychologists have for long been concerned with seeking an optimal relationship between man and job, but have tended historically to concentrate on the areas of personnel selection, placement and training. Jaques brings the pay element into the picture, having first studied problems of equilibrium between pay and work, introducing capacity later.

Jaques discerns in individual consumption patterns, individual capacities and levels of income, homeostatic relationships. The point is that individuals differ in their capacities for performing different levels of work, in their present capacities, and in their potential capacities. The potential capacity of any individual shows a characteristic developmental pattern over time; it rises and falls with age. Individuals have an unconscious awareness of what their capacities for work are, and what their level of remuneration should be. They seek jobs which satisfy their capacities, which provide an appropriate level of remuneration, and so satisfy their spending habits. Individuals whose capacities are well-adjusted to the level of work they do, and where work provides them with a subjectively felt equitable level of payment are said to be in a state of 'psycho-economic' equilibrium.

Jaques postulates that when the level of work is measured by 'time-span', a general and universal pay structure can be established. To the extent that payment for jobs is consistent with the structure, so will incumbents in those jobs be satisfied with the payments received. Jaques dichotomises work into 'prescribed' and 'discretionary' activities. The discretionary aspect is the more important. For this there is a current time-span capacity (time-span capacity at an individual's current age) and a potential time-span capacity (his maximum time-span in the future). Individuals press towards finding work at a level

100

commensurate with their current time-span capacity in order to maximise their satisfaction. The 'discretionary' activities are defined as those aspects of a work-role about which a subordinate must exercise his own discretion, rather than follow laid-down rules and procedures, in order to execute his function satisfactorily. The 'time-span of discretion' is 'the longest period of time which can elapse in a role before a superior can be sure that his subordinate has not been exercising marginally substandard discretion continuously in balancing the pace and quality of his work' (Jaques, 1964). The theory applies only to certain types of economic work directed to the production of goods and services for which a contract of employment has been entered into. It excludes directing and entrepreneurial aspects, the risk-taking activities of shareholders, all forms of self-employment and non-economic work.

Jaques relates the concept of 'equity theory' (see Chapter 2) with the 'time-span of discretion'. 'Equitable payment' is the common norm which people in roles of the same time-span, when asked in confidence, indicate they would consider to be fair pay. 'Equitable payment' is sometimes referred to as 'felt-fair pay'. Felt-fair norms of pay include total emoluments, such as fringe benefits, company cars and the like, and are independent of the amount of income-tax paid or number of hours worked. Jaques claims high correlations between 'time-span' and norms of 'felt-fair pay' based on research at Glacier Metal during the period 1954–62, where a relationship was observed between the time-span of discretion of work in a job and the worker's intuitive judgement about what was the fair pay for the work he was given to do, irrespective of the reasons he might produce in support of his judgement. Eight years of research at Glacier produced correlations of roughly 0·90 between felt-fair pay and time-span measurement. Research in the USA, conducted at the Honeywell Company under the technical supervision of the University of Minnesota, in the personages of Professor Mahoney of the department of labour economics and Professor Dunnette of the department of industrial psychology, investigated felt-fair pay in relation to some thirty variables, including time-span, actual pay, five job evaluation factors, and market rates. They found a 0·85 correlation between time-span and felt-fair pay, a correlation of 0·40 between job evaluation factors and felt-fair pay, and a correlation of 0·20 between market rates and felt-fair pay. Time-span measurements obtained separately from boss and subordinate correlated at over 0·90;

the job evaluation factors only in the 0·40s (Jaques, 1969). Further research in the UK at Brunel University, not confined to a single firm, but investigating nearly a dozen industrial and government organisations, has produced correlations of 0·83 between time-span and felt-fair pay (Evans, 1970). The indication is that employers share ideas about fair rewards for work with different levels of responsibility, and that time-span is the common element of work which gives rise to a comparative sense of fairness. As at the 1970 earnings index, one could approximately say, for example, that a time-span of one day merited an annual gross payment of £1,265, a time-span of six months merited £2,010 and eighteen months merited £3,500 (Evans, 1970) based on felt-fair conceptions.

How norms are established is much less clear. They seem to be built up through a process of comparing one's own capacity and job against other people's, and eventually, subconsciously, a framework of knowledge is built up about other occupations and roles, even if one's own experience of the work involved has only been vicarious or indirect. Feelings of dissatisfaction with pay are due not only to comparisons giving invidious results, but also from maladjustments in the C-W-P trio, or from dissatisfaction with one's living standard generally vis-à-vis the national economic situation. Jaques claims that the differential pattern between individuals as regards capacities, pay and work itself gives rise to norms of equity. It is posited that a normative distribution of skills, of work roles, and therefore of equitable payments exists. One of the important contentions is that violations from the norm can give rise to discomfort (neurotic disequilibrium), and Jaques goes so far at one point as to suggest that it can be a cause of war(!) More specifically, 'individuals whose actual payment bracket remains within ±3 per cent of equity, tend to express themselves as feeling that their role is being reasonably paid relative to others' (Jaques, 1961). Apparently, at ±5 per cent feelings of uneasiness appear, at −10 per cent these become even stronger, whilst at +10 per cent the overpaid incumbent will suffer feelings of guilt. 'At about 20 per cent departure from equity an explosive situation develops, the outcome of which would be difficult to predict' (Jaques, 1967).

The existence of norms is not instantly recognisable. Norms are unconscious and intuitive, and do not come to the surface in the course of normal conversation. They are deep-rooted, intuitive judgements. So

102

much for the professed objectivity of the theory. Moreover, they can only be discovered in a private 'social-analytical' interview. Jaques cannot adduce any evidence to account for the normative conceptions, but the hypothesis is that the equitable work payment scale must be positively sloped because individuals differ in their capacity to exercise discrimination in their spending and therefore in the level of consumption which gives rise to satisfaction, and an individual's consumption satisfaction is associated with his capacity to carry responsibility at work. In the Glacier experiment, workers held a positive relationship in their minds between the time-span of discretion in a job and what they felt was fair pay for the work involved. If differences in individual capacities for work and in patterns for consumption-satisfaction distribute themselves normally in a population, there is in theory, therefore, a corresponding optimal normal distribution of income which would best fit the natural distribution of talents and temperaments which gravitate to work-roles of appropriate time-span. 'The totality of these norms constitutes a pattern of equitable payment for differentials in levels of work carried' (Jaques, 1961).

The measurement of time-span can be rather nebulous. It is not as straightforward as the theory suggests. Apart from the neglect of humdrum work of a routine nature, the problem is to determine how substandard discretion of the incumbent will come to the manager's notice. Review may be relatively immediate—or even direct—but in most cases it is indirect in that the boss tends to let the work pass without appraisal on the assumption that any indiscretion exercised which is substandard will in the fullness of time come to light when the results of the subordinate's efforts are used or acted upon in another part of the organisation. In any case, the boss is too busy to vet everything, or there would be no point in delegation. The determination of substandard discretion for any item of work is based on successive approximation and is a marginal concept—i.e. mistakes and misadventures which are immediately apparent are not included if they concern isolated tasks; included only is substandard discretion of which the effect would be cumulative. A *sine qua non* is that the manager himself is not exercising substandard discretion and can therefore detect and discriminate between behaviours of subordinates. For the scheme to have any semblance of reliability, all managers at a given level must be in agreement about standards of performance and be

103

able to evaluate accordingly—a tall order. Clearly, also, the nature of time-span as defined will depend upon organisational variables such as structure, reporting and control systems, deadlines and so forth, determined quite independently from the level of work a particular individual happens to be doing in the organisation. Another point is that Jaques, lacking an independent method of estimating an individual's time-span capacity, but having noted in his interviews that satisfaction from equilibrium (or vice versa) was obtained, inferred that capacity was matched to level of work and to payment. Unfortunately, this is an assumption of the theory and not an empirical verification. Time-span capacity, if not substantiated, is no more than a hypothetical construct. Whilst there may indeed be evidence to suggest a correlation with time-span of discretion and felt-fair pay (itself a subjective phenomenon for which there is no supporting theory) there is no proof of any relationship between time-span and individual capacity. The differential demands made on a job incumbent are more likely to be determined by organisational structure than by the latent capacities of the employee. Jaques circumvents this type of problem by admitting that time-span capacities are not static but change over time. In his schemata, coupled with current conceptions of time-span et al., are ideas about the future.

Jaques has developed the idea of 'capacity growth curves' (referred to in his earlier literature as 'standard earnings progressions'). The implications are that each individual intuitively knows the rate of development of his capacity, and that characteristically, there is a process of growth and decline with age. It is possible, therefore, to plot a continuous family of curves of earnings against age for the population as a whole, and particularly for those in 'equilibrium'. If there is an unconscious awareness of (a) current potential capacity for work, (b) level of work in a role, (c) equitable payment for that work, this can be true for any individual at any point in time at any stage of his career. One simply then has to look at an individual, say A at age thirty, find someone of like capacity at a later stage of development, say B at age fifty-five, and assuming they remain in equilibrium, and allowing for adjustments in inflation and the value of money, one can predict that A will be earning the equivalent of what B is now in twenty-five years' time when he has himself reached age fifty-five. If, for some reason, things do not quite work out like that, A will become frustrated, guilty, unhappy, suicidal or whatever. 'One of the basic assumptions which led to the construction of the capacity growth curves was that individuals would seek an equitable level of payment for the level of work they were capable of carrying' (Jaques, 1967). Diagramatically the idea can be presented as in Figure 6.1. The curve (i.e. smooth progression) for an individual can be ascertained by finding that point where his levels of work and payment are in equilibrium according to age. The snag is, of course, that since there is no way of measuring

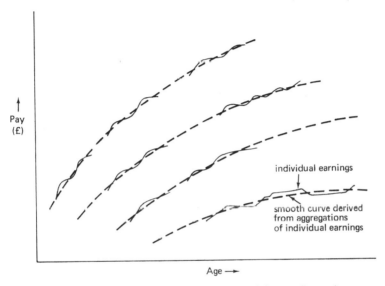

Fig. 6.1 Capacity Growth Curves (after E. Jaques)

capacity (although Goodman (1967) tried to develop one) one must hazard a guess at it operationally in the form of what Jaques calls a 'potential progress assessment'. The crystal-ball gazing here is no different from that which goes into any career development consideration. What is more important is that although earnings progressions certainly exist, and many an organisation spends time plotting them on historical data to get a bird's-eye view of how career progression has been panning out, so that the graphs stand out like iron filings in a magnetic field, there is absolutely no statistical rationale why they should in fact do so. The pretty patterns of serendipity have no psychological

105

basis either. The progression of individual development is not necessarily uniform or unidirectional. Jaques's determinism has the air of a self-fulfilling prophecy. Having once got on to a curve it may be difficult to get off it. The prophecy would appear to be fulfilled. In reality extrapolation is highly tenuous and complex. Opportunities, organisational change, growth or contraction, transfer earnings and the mobility of labour are the variables, the whims of fate, over which control cannot be exercised. Earnings progressions relate to length of service, possibly to age, to merit, the level of work performed and responsibility held and the degree of confidence which the organisation is prepared to invest in the individual. From data on earnings progressions in the US, Laner and Caplan (1969) found a linear (rather than logarithmic) regression of earnings with age, with the slope of the curve (regression coefficient) *unrelated* to initial earnings. Projection may well be deception. At best Jaques's curves must be treated as hypothetical constructs rather than quantitative results.

A further facet to the theory is Jaques' observation of the existence of ranks or clearly discernible hierarchical levels in the relative importance of time-spans in an organisation as a whole, an idea later taken up and developed by T. T. Paterson. Jaques has been able to group jobs of different time-spans into categories. Basically he identifies five main ranks, ranging from Rank 1 (with less than one month's time-span) through to Rank 5 (with a time-span of over five years). In very large organisations Ranks 6 and 7 may exist, the latter having a time-span of over twenty years. The observation is probably of more operational consequence for Paterson, whom we shall discuss later. Jaques' observation largely reflects the tendency of organisations to build their structures on hierarchical criteria and the main precept is that the organisation of work is of more fundamental importance than devising an elaborate labyrinth of career avenues and associated pay levels. The point is that if organisation is got right in terms of responsibility levels, a natural structure of grades emerges conforming with time-spans of discretion and the solution to pay is axiomatic. Predetermination of ranks, however, poses an absolute criterion of organisational design, which taken across the wide range of industry, technology and commerce would seem to be spurious.

The theory is complex and far-reaching. It is intellectually fascinating and constitutes a whole social philosophy. From the job evaluation point of view, the tenet is simple enough: the discretionary content of work constitutes the real burden, and about this people hold unconscious norms of its monetary value which correlate with the amount of time which can elapse before substandard performance becomes evident. If you can therefore measure these time-lags, you have the key to an equitable system of payment applicable to all jobs. The extension of Jaques' argument is that time-span could be used nationally, even internationally, as the foundation of a systematic payment structure which people would accept as just and fair because it would be based on measurement and cut out bargaining and wage pressure groups. Yet the incidence of the Jaques technique is marginal in the extreme. Why?

Precisely because it undermines traditional strategies for the resolution of conflict, institutionalised bargaining powers, it has received short shrift. Even at Glacier Metal, the adoption of the scheme was rejected by the works council. Modern industrial society is one essentially founded upon sectionalised interests operating in a climate of distrust and suspicion. Apart from the problem of dispersing conditioned attitudes, to gain acceptance of a change so new and radical would demand of the panacea presented absolute perfection. Ideas about socially acceptable pay are not new; they are Aristotelian in origin. In principle the ideas are probably acceptable; the means for achieving them are controversial. Jaques substitutes grand theorem for corporate stratagem. The perceived risks are too great. Moreover, the moths have got at the theory; bits of it are left in shreds. How can, for example, social cohesion result from the time-span of discretion theory if entrepreneurial work and self-employment are ignored? What about chores of a routine, manual nature consisting predominantly of prescribed duties? How are they to be compensated? The problem is that he seeks reliance on a segmental, single factor of job evaluation. This is the main ground for its unacceptability and where conventional job evaluation techniques have greater face validity. But the cry goes up: these are too subjective! Instead, reveal to Jaques your innermost feelings. This must surely be the zenith of pseudo-scientific objectivity. What is more, since the psychoanalytical technique requires special training, we have a new and esoteric band-waggon to boot. What about conspect reliability between analysts? No evidence from Jaques, but some from Richardson (1971), none of it conclusive. Indeed, throughout, there is a lack of adequate empirical evidence to support the theory.

107

Jaques postulates a neat constellation of constructs—he may well be right—but unfortunately he cannot prove it. Proof is partly denied by difficulty of measuring basic parameters like satisfaction, capacity, equity. At worst we end up with a circular argument, at best with an unsubstantiated hypothesis. Jaques does not know how or why time-span measures level of work or embodies the essence of equity, but somehow it seems to, and there it stands, lacking statistical analysis or any form of coherent quantitative treatment. Managers are sceptical of scientific laws anyway, preferring to act by heuristic visional hypotheses. Data based on psychoanalytical investigations into the pathology of normative values do not enthuse them. Their acceptance is a major problem and their lack of credence even makes inroads into further experimentation difficult. Apart from aspersions which may be cast on its validity, Jaques' system faces so many political and administrative difficulties, it is likely to remain a theoretical contribution to the payment problem rather than have any practical application.

DECISION-BANDING

The idea of a common yardstick applicable to the evaluation of jobs of all types and levels has been taken up by Professor T. T. Paterson of the University of Strathclyde in a series of monographs and finally in book form (Paterson, 1972). Paterson chides economists for their failure adequately to explain differentials, and attributes poor industrial relations mainly to the lack of a coherent theory for determining relative differences in pay. He believes, like Jaques, that management has a major responsibility for job evaluation and similarly accepts the principles of equity and justice. He criticises conventional techniques on the grounds of their subjectivity, arbitrary methods of analysis, frequent inappropriateness and inability to compare unlike jobs with theoretical validity. Instead, he proposes a scheme which uses a single factor, namely 'decision making'. This one factor is, to a greater or lesser extent, a common criterion for all jobs; it has universality. 'The common denominator from tea boy to chairman is quality of decision' (Paterson, 1969). Potentially, it provides a unitary basis for comparing jobs throughout the employment range, across firms and across industries.

'It is recognised that there will always be some subjectively decided elements in a man's *earnings* (as distinct from pay)—he is rewarded more, for example, for working in bad conditions, he is given extra because of his long and faithful service. But it is the job content that has the basic value, not the skill brought to it, or the effort expended, or the environmental conditions. All these can be and must be regarded as subjectively estimated and added to, *marginal* to the job content, for which the *base rate* is *pay* (as distinct from earnings). Skills change as people change, conditions and effort alter as technology alters, people leave or die and seniority disappears. The base rate of a task is, or should be constant, and objectively determinable in order to establish fair differential, and, very important, the same criteria for determining base rate should be used for all jobs, shop floor, office, managerial, laboratory, drawing office. There should be no room for the accusations of double standards—one for managers and one for "workers"' (Paterson, 1969).

Simply stated, Paterson's approach to job evaluation involves four main stages:

1. Establishment of job bands according to decision type and structure
2. Job analysis—examining the content of jobs
3. Job grading and subgrading—the ranking of jobs
4. Job assessment—ascribing monetary values.

Job bands are broad generic categories of work according to the type and level of decision made. Like time-span, the significant difference between jobs is indicated by the quality of decision. Paterson's contention is that every known job can be considered and compared against six basic levels of decision making, thus:

Band E: Policy-making decisions, made by top management
Band D: Programming decisions, made by senior management in the execution of policy
Band C: Interpretive decisions, made by middle management (e.g. departmental heads) within the limits set at Band D on what is to be done
Band B: Routine decisions, made by skilled operators concerning the execution of interpreted policy and the processes involved
Band A: Automatic decisions, made by semi-skilled operators on the operational aspects of the process such as 'when', 'how' and 'where' to do something
Band O: Defined decisions, made by unskilled workers.

Resulting from job analysis, the decision-making content of jobs can be determined, and the job itself placed in the appropriate band. Life is not quite as simple as that, however, for the bands, as has been stated, are broad generic groups, and considerable subdivision of function is contained within them. For example, within any one level of job, a certain task may have particular difficulty or be more important. Paterson proposes a *decision count* which considers work of 'relative complexity' or 'relative importance'. This is easier if decisions can in fact be counted and if there are clearly specified tasks, which might obtain for bands O, A, B, and where regular decisions are made at specific intervals. Alternatively, a more subjective *count-ranking* technique may be applied, a mixture of counting and ranking, or simply conventional *ranking* to determine the relative importance in decision making between jobs. Paterson's advocacy and implementation of these techniques is rather abstruse, but the point of this finer analysis is that bands may be broken down into grades, and further 'a grade may be divided into subgrades in order to provide differentials that indicate, in greater detail, differences in value of the job' (Paterson, 1972). The classification becomes more complex.

'The concept of decision bands can be further refined in the organisation structure. Each decision band, except Band O, is divided into two levels or grades, upper and lower. The upper-level job holder in any decision band co-ordinates the work of the men in the lower level of the same decision band; he is the line-manager of the lower level worker in the same band. Thus, for example, the upper level of Band B is the decision level of the shop foreman. His function is to co-ordinate the work of his subordinates, and he can therefore be seen as a manager in the accepted sense. On the other hand, the foreman is not widely accepted as a manager, simply because he does not decide why certain action should be taken' (Paterson and Husband, 1970).

Within a band, the person in the upper grade co-ordinates the work of those in the lower grade and has 'structural' authority over them. Similarly, each band has 'structural' authority over the band immediately below it. Eleven hierarchical grades indicate the relative value of work to the organisation, and there is scope for grades to be further broken down into subgrades according to the lowest, middle and highest levels of decision making. Band E has two grades, and the other bands A, B, C, D, O collectively comprise twenty-three possible subgrades. Work study techniques may facilitate subgrading in the lowest bands O and A, and Paterson suggests points assessments for subgrading for band B, and ranking for bands C and D. Subgrades are determined as a percentage of the total decisions made, albeit often according to subjective assessment.

The important finding from the application of the Paterson method is that when current rates of basic pay for jobs evaluated by the method are plotted on a log scale on the Y axis and the equidistant grades on the X axis, the line of best fit which emerges is usually straight. Pay differentials between grades increase exponentially, the percentage increase in average basic pay between each grade being more or less constant. From a wide variety of applications over a range of organisations in different countries, including Europe, India and South Africa, first begun in the latter in 1961, 'taken as a whole, the total sample shows that the general theory holds, that differentials tend to be based upon a decision-making grading from unskilled jobs to the board-room, with an exponential increase from Grade to Grade' (Paterson, 1972). Support seems to be lent to Jaques' principle of time-span of discretion, at least within a firm. The gradient tends to vary between industries and between firms. Larger, and higher paying firms, tend to have steeper gradients. Labour scarcities can cause departures from the straight line, and likewise poor industrial relations and disputes over pay differentials can cause deviations.

Paterson claims that this method is based on consensual agreement, through formally structured grading and assessment committees composed of management and union representatives, or representatives of non-unionised employees where necessary. He believes it embodies the principles of trade unionism, of equality and equity. There is no formal grievance procedure, and in fact the system is rather rigid. The traditional assumptions about industrial remuneration are built into the system. People are paid according to their position in the hierarchy and the *status quo* is underwritten. Differential rewards are strictly maintained, modified only by the slope of the pay curve. Although in theory the method can provide a common denominator, wide discrepancies are found between firms and across industries. Mainly this is due to concentration on base rates. Allowance is made for the negotiation of 'contingency' payments, e.g. overtime, special premiums, etc.,

111

as additions to the basic rate. In real life, earnings are more important than basic rates in order to accommodate local labour market scarcities and are in part influenced by relative bargaining powers, company profitability and ability to pay. The system is therefore in danger of building a two-tier structure and of perpetuating the contemporary phenomenon of wage drift. Paterson's claim that it can provide a basis for incomes policy (*The Times*, 6 March 1972) is refutable, notwithstanding the merit of deriving basic rates from common criteria. What the scheme does offer is a uniform classification system which could be applied universally. The inflexibility of classification systems has already been commented on. Moreover, operationally, a central weakness of the method is that it relies, despite the rigorous training recommended, on the judgement of one man—the job analyst. Questions of conspect reliability between analysts and raters are not entered into, let alone answered. Some of the actual techniques used for subgrading are, inevitably, rather subjective. Certainly they are recondite, and one would suspect not always comprehensible to the working man. True, the system has been applied with reported success in the Rhodesian Civil Service, was recommended by the National Board for Prices and Incomes for the nursing profession, and has been experimented with by the British Steel Corporation. But the Achilles' heel of the method is that one of the principles on which it rests is fallacious. Because the outcome conforms with existing pay rates, it does not mean to say that they are the right ones. They do not validate the scheme.

DIRECT CONSENSUS METHOD

The direct consensus method has been developed by Associated Industrial Consultants Ltd and has now been applied successfully at various levels from manual workers to supervisory and technical positions in a range of industries, including engineering, furniture manufacture and electronics, on a consultancy basis. As the name implies, it is founded upon consensus, but also jointly upon the system of paired comparison. Conceptually, the idea owes something to Elliott Jaques' ideas about felt-fair pay. In a working environment the hypothesis is that a certain 'conventional wisdom' exists about the relationships between various jobs and hence about questions of pay differentials. The predetermination of key criteria against which to assess jobs, as in a points system, is eschewed. Instead, if there are in fact any key criteria common and relevant to a range of jobs, they are determined by a cross-sampling of opinion and statistical analysis. The first steps are conventional enough. Job descriptions are prepared from a representative sample of jobs in the survey. For technical reasons the number of jobs chosen should be a prime number between eleven and seventy-nine. A representative committee of assessors must also be established, and again for technical reasons, the number of assessors must be geared to the number of jobs to be evaluated, so that each assessor ranks an equal percentage of the total. The number of assessors tends to be larger than is normal under a points rating system and every considered judgement is taken into account. Mathematically, the number of paired comparisons which will be made is roughly proportional to the square of the number of jobs in the sample. Operationally, jobs are ranked on the basis of paired comparisons. All possible combinations of pairs are included. If N is the number of jobs, the number of comparisons is

$$\frac{N(N-1)}{2},$$ so that if eleven jobs are chosen there would be fifty-five

comparisons. Pre-printed forms are provided by the consultants indicating the pairs of jobs to be ranked as 'wholes' on the overall criterion of job importance. The combined rankings of all judges are fed into a computer to determine the overall rank order and the degree of agreement between assessors. Discrepancies and anomalies must be reconsidered. The computer print-out may or may not indicate general guidelines as to natural breaks in the hierarchy which may be used for grade demarcations. In any case, this can be a matter for discussion. The original pairings against the criterion of job importance may provide sufficient dispersion against which to rank the remaining jobs. Alternatively, the assessors may repeat the comparisons indicating their preferences under factor headings. A factor plan can also be used in cases where assessors have been unable to agree about jobs in their preliminary rankings. Factor plans in fact should be developed if future changes in job content are envisaged. To avoid some of the arbitrariness in establishing factor plans, the statistical technique of multiple regression analysis can be used to ensure that the relative weighting of factors conforms with the consensus of opinion and requirements of the organisation. The facility of a computer is clearly vital in dealing with so many details of opinion and judgement. It also has the added advantage that it can be used to cost the system and produce various permutations for the possible distribution of corporate wealth. The actual pricing of the structure is open to company policy, negotiation and comparison of market rates.

GUIDE-CHART PROFILE METHOD

Another method developed by a firm of management consultants, Hay-MSL Ltd, and available to individual organisations on a consultancy basis, is the Guide-Chart Profile Method. Its operational distinction is that it attempts to combine job evaluation with external comparison of market rates as a unified package. Applicable mainly to managerial, administrative and executive jobs, it compares the relative importance of salaried jobs to each other and to total organisational objectives. In a way it is a modification of the point method, and since its inception (Hay and Purves, 1951) it has undergone considerable refinements, and the current methodology has evolved from the study of management jobs in client companies. One of its main tenets is that a measure of *accountability* exists in any management job. In other words, a job has a purpose, and objectives can be set in relation to organisational goals. The importance of objectives may vary from job to job, and similarly, the degree to which they are accomplished successfully may vary from one incumbent to another. The concept of accountability is a common factor. Apart from this measure of accountability, successful performance will also require a degree of knowledge and experience, termed *know-how*, in order to analyse problems and come to conclusions about appropriate courses of action, and an inherent job factor termed *problem solving*. These three aspects are the key elements in any managerial job, and when evaluated on these lines, a profile of each job can be constructed for the purposes of inter- and intra-organisational comparison. Guide charts developed for firms by Hay-MSL indicate graduated standards for making evaluations and building up profiles. The exact details of the scheme are copyright, but we can look at its underlying principles.

The main input which an incumbent brings to his job is know-how, characterised by two broad aspects: (*a*) skill, education and training, (*b*) breadth of management know-how, including such facets as planning,

114

organising, co-ordinating, etc. Each of these broad aspects may be divided into a number of degrees indicating variations in the input required. The two outputs which ensue from the performance of a job role are accountability and problem solving. Problem solving is concerned with the frequency, importance and complexity of problems and the thought processes required, and is divided into (a) the thinking environment, i.e. the constraints of the organisation in terms of rules, procedures, policies, etc., and (b) the thinking challenge, which is the nature of mental processes, whether routine, repetitive, analytical, creative, etc. Again, each subfactor is divided into degrees. Accountability is concerned with the results obtained and the value of resources controlled. It is divided into the two broad headings of: (a) freedom to act, (b) magnitude of accountability. Degrees are again applied.

In summary, for the factors of know-how and accountability, points scales are allocated, while problem solving is treated as a percentage of the know-how deployed. Operationally, each job is rated under each criterion, and jobs can be plotted on charts to show up the job structure in quantitative terms. For example, a job profile would show the relationship between inputs and outputs, the relationship between the individual human resources necessary (know-how) to tackle the job, the amount of thought required (problem solving) and the results obtained (accountability). Further, they help to show up the balance between 'thought' and 'action' within any job—i.e. 'advisory' as distinct from 'decision making'—and also between types of job in any organisation. Professor T. T. Paterson (1972) quotes from some private notes he received from W. F. Younger of Hay-MSL:

'In essence the Hay Guide-Chart Profile method is concerned with providing a common language to describe the relationships which exist between different roles in any organisation. This common language allows people who are knowledgeable about the roles under consideration to come to a consensus judgement of the relative significance of the different roles in that particular environment.'

The language referred to is a geometric scale to which the evaluated scores on the three dimensions are converted. For example, Job X

Know-How	528
Problem Solving (50% K.H.)	264
Accountability	400
	1192

produces a geometric profile of 44.22.34 (total 100 per cent) for that particular job, one having a high degree of accountability. Differences between jobs can be clearly indicated in this fashion. The final part of the package is that jobs in a firm having been evaluated by this method can be compared to the (copyrighted distribution) of market rates for salaries for outside jobs—presumably ones which have been evaluated by the same method. The scheme is a detailed analytical, quantitative technique. It is partly an adaptation of points rating and bears some resemblance both to time-span and decision-banding in that it is partly a measurement of the man in the job. Its usage is fairly widespread. In the UK it has been used in at least part of a number of major companies, including EMI, ICI, Unilever, Hawker Siddeley and Sperry Rand, and internationally has found application in Europe, America, Australia and Africa.

URWICK ORR PROFILE METHOD

Another method of job evaluation under the title of job profiling was originated by management consultants Urwick Orr and Partners Ltd in 1960. Names can be misleading and the scheme bears virtually no similarity to the Hay-MSL technique of profiling. It is certainly far less abstruse. Rather, if anything, it is more akin to direct consensus of AIC, although at root it is a combination of points rating and ranking. The Urwick Orr scheme is particularly worthy of note because of its adaptability, its participative approach and its proven acceptability in large-scale enterprise. Two of its main UK applications have been in the Ford Motor Company and the British Steel Corporation.

In the steel industry, following upon renationalisation, a need was felt to rationalise wage and salary structures throughout the corporation. Initially, a pilot study with the agreement of the Trades Union Congress Steel Industry Consultative Committee, was carried out at the Normanby Park works in the Scunthorpe Group. The purpose of this exercise was not specifically to alter wage structures, but simply to test the feasibility and viability of the scheme in an integrated works to gain some first-hand experience of operating the scheme on a joint management/union co-operative basis and elicit reactions from work-folk.

Conforming with common practice, bench mark jobs are first selected representative of the range of jobs under consideration, and are rated according to six generic factors: responsibility, knowledge, mental demands, social demands, physical demands, and work environment. Each generic factor is scored on a four-point scale (basic, moderate, high, exceptional). According to the work situation a number of sub-factors may also be employed, but essentially the scheme is kept simple and understandable, ignoring minor differences in work and concentrating only on the basic differences between jobs. Bench mark jobs are then placed in rank order according to their total score values. The jobs are then reranked on a 'whole' job basis, and the two sets of results compared and reconciled. Where discrepancies occur, these may be removed by reconsidering the weighting of subfactors until a workable and acceptable framework emerges. This takes the form of making paired comparisons of unweighted jobs on the four-point scale and feeding the data into a computer to determine the weightings that would best fit the ratings obtained by paired comparison. Jobs are presented as a profile of points scores. The points scoring system is commendably straightforward. Moreover, a high degree of consultation is the hall-mark of the scheme. Works steering committees of union representatives and management have overall control of the exercise. In the Normanby Park study four members of the national joint working party were also included to provide liaison between the pilot study itself and general matters of job evaluation being considered by a joint working party nationally. In the work situation assessors comprise a central reviewing committee (at Normanby Park called a joint assessment committee) representative of the various interested parties and including a consultant from Urwick Orr. The consultants undertake to train members of the central review committee in problems of assessment and profiling.

The steel industry is complicated both technologically and in the co-ordination of its multisite activities. It also has some sixteen trade unions to contend with. The Normanby Park study was a trial run concentrating on manual workers. Following upon its success, a further shot was had at middle management jobs with a view to establishing a national salary structure. Accordingly the corporation and the Steel Industry Management Association set up a joint working party in 1970 to test-run the Urwick Orr profile method at the Stocksbridge and Tinsley Park Works of the Special Steels Division. Satisfied with the results, agreement was reached in 1971 to adopt the scheme throughout the corporation on a national front.

117

Ford's adoption was an earlier, and probably bigger, success in that the company decided in 1966 to replace a system of payment for 40,000 workers, which had existed since 1949 with an unfortunate record of labour disputes, by a productivity bargain based on Urwick Orr's job evaluation scheme, involving negotiation with twenty-two unions in twenty-three plants. For the purpose fifty-six bench mark jobs were selected, the bare minimum necessary to cover the full range of operations. In passing, it is interesting to note that even more bench mark jobs were utilised in British Steel's application, where fifty-two were selected for manual jobs and seventy for middle management jobs. The upshot of the Ford scheme for manual workers was that five new grades were established, with an earnings progression between them replacing the previously traditional demarcations of skilled, semi-skilled and unskilled, a system under which 80 per cent of production workers were classed as semi-skilled and paid the same rate. One of the important aspects of Ford's implementation of job evaluation was the high degree of consultation at every stage of the development between management and unions. A second point is that it was possible to adapt Urwick Orr's factor complex, by a minor addition, to fit organisational needs. Most impressive is the speed with which the exercise was carried out. Perhaps this was partly because the unions had been offered an $11\frac{1}{2}$ per cent increase in wages spread over two years as part of the productivity pact. It was an ambitious and complicated project, with many related concomitant issues such as the scrapping of merit awards and substitution of service increments, so that the exact contribution of Urwick Orr's profiling technique is difficult to disentangle.

Chapter 7

Theoretical Considerations

It would be remiss, even in a book devoted primarily to the practical applications of job evaluation, to ignore some of the more important theoretical considerations. Some of these have been referred to in passing in the previous discussions, but this chapter attempts to draw the main threads together. The acceptability in practice of job evaluation as a determinant of income, and no less its acceptability in theory, must depend on its reliability and validity. Employees and rigorous theoreticians alike will jibe at a system which is neither consistent nor accurate. The concepts of reliability and validity are fundamental to almost any technique in occupational psychology, and therefore by extension to aspects of personnel management aimed at obtaining optimal relationships between man, job and working environment. Validity is concerned with accuracy, with the extent to which an instrument does in fact measure what it purports to measure. Reliability is a measure of consistency; it is a measure of the extent to which results are reproducible. In job evaluation, a reliable system would be one which produced the same outcome at a different point in time (assuming the content of jobs had not changed) with the same (or different) group of assessors applying the same set of measuring instruments. Rarely does one find instruments which are perfectly reliable.

Disparity between judgements undermines the reliability of ratings. This danger was first recognised by Barth (1921), an early pioneer of work study. Not only might assessors using the same rating-factors disagree between themselves, but there might also be inconsistencies in ratings made by the same analyst from day to day. The recurring question of the reliability of subjective estimates has not adequately been resolved since Uhrbrock's (1935) important study in which he reported that six judges, using a ten-point scale, independently rated twenty-three men on quality of output. Correlations between the ratings of two judges proved to be approximately 0·40 and of two independent sets of three judges, 0·63. Neither level of agreement can be considered satisfactory. The problem is still with us. Even, of course, if there is consistently a high level of agreement between judges, it does not mean to say that the judgement is necessarily correct. This is a question of validity.

The main cause of variance is due to error and bias in human judgement. Job evaluation is not scientific. Although its methodology may be logical, it is not provable nor is its outcome predictable. It is all a matter of subjective judgement. What we would ideally wish from our judges are qualities and abilities which one might well regard as superhuman. Primarily we want agreement (i.e. reliability). We want them in the present situation to be consistent between themselves in their assessments (conspect reliability or interrater reliability). We would want them also to be able to agree in the future, to be able to repeat their assessments, to demonstrate a high co-efficient of stability. We would also ideally want them to be able to come to the same conclusions if they were obliged to make their assessments by some other technique (co-efficient of equivalence). A very tall order indeed. Where one is using objective measurements such things are possible. With human, subjective measurements they very rarely are. Why not?

The mental processes of judgement in individual assessors are highly variable. Assessors will hold different standards upon which their judgement is based, and these will have been determined by their individual backgrounds, training and experience. Although common standards can be laid down, preconceived notions will still affect judgement. Mahler (1950), investigating sound judgement in merit rating schemes, for example, found that the more important attributes were 'the ability to judge' and 'the willingness to judge'. Ability was influenced by adequate opportunity to observe the subject, by an awareness of the need to rate, and by the suitability of the rating scheme. The willingness to judge was a function of an assessor's understanding of the programme, his acceptance of its aims, and his attitude towards management. Clearly, people are not identical. Another relevant study, by Taft (1962) into the qualities necessary for good judgement, suggested three main attributes, namely, possession of appropriate judgement norms, the ability to judge, and motivation. Taft found that a high degree of motivation on the part of assessors to secure reliable judgements was the most important quality. Taft also found that the 'ability to judge' correlated with general and social intelligence, while 'judgement norms' depended on an assessor's having a similar background to the subject. It is not surprising therefore that disagreement can arise.

One of the most common manifestations of subjective judgement exhibits itself in 'halo effect', so named after Thorndike's constant error (1920). People tend to focus their attention on the most demonstrative aspects of an individual, positive or negative, and the same phenomenon applies in any subjective assessment. While it is perfectly true, and cannot be overemphasised, that job evaluation is concerned with an evaluation of the job and not of the incumbent, two problems stand out. One is that it is the most important aspects of a job, good or bad, difficult or easy, which catch attention, and the other is that it is sometimes impossible not to be influenced by the person actually doing the job and his (her) particular commendable (disreputable) attributes. Judgement is a subjective process, and this is a fact we are faced with. There is also the problem of 'central tendency'. In making ratings there is a natural tendency to avoid using extreme scores at either end of the range, partly because one may be called to account for, and substantiate, extreme decisions. The result is bunching in the centre. For example, when using a five-point scale, the first and fifth points are the most neglected. Discrimination becomes even less of a fine art, and more of a political nicety. Forced distribution can overcome these problems, under which assessors are obliged to spread their ratings in accordance with a predetermined pattern, normally on the assumption of a chi-squared distribution. But of course the assumption may well not be valid in measuring a range of jobs, and the people performing them have probably been specially selected anyway.

Judgement may be further adversely affected by differences in status between assessors. Elliot (1960) has shown that the opinions of a senior assessor considerably influence the judgement of the others. In the Elliot study, job evaluation panels assessed the relative position of shorthand typists and cost clerks under nine factors. Eight separate panels were concerned with the evaluation. In four of them the chairmen were instructed to suggest that the typist should be rated higher. In the

121

other four panels the chairmen were instructed to suggest that the clerks be rated higher. After deliberation, the considered verdict of all the assessors conformed with the views of their respective chairmen. The degree of influence may have differed from one chairman to another, and the relative balance of scores awarded to typists and clerks varied, but the final result does seem to suggest that people are particularly gullible, amenable or obedient in hierarchical situations. It is of course a common observation that both formal and informal leaders always exert some influence in group decision making. There would seem to be a need for aiming at a balanced status amongst assessors, maybe coupled with a rotation of the chairmanship role. Perhaps too, in this particular instance, the panels would have got nearer the truth if the typists and clerks had been allowed to speak for themselves. There is certainly a moral case to be made out for people whose jobs are being evaluated to be represented on the assessment panel. The excuse of hiding behind the administrative practicalities can become a source of invalidity.

Training can partly overcome deficiencies. Chesler (1948) reports that raters who had been trained, assessed thirty-five jobs, and achieved high reliability co-efficients ranging from 0·93 to 0·99. Similarly, people improve with practice, and there is some evidence to suggest that experience in handling a particular technique leads to speedier, more consistent, results. However, it does not mean to say that the skills acquired thereby are automatically transferred to the use of another technique. Partly, too, possible faults can be controlled by using established psychological procedures, such as the pooling of rankings of several raters to obtain averages, or by the method of paired comparisons (for jobs or factors). The number of individuals needed to provide ratings before the final rating, or average, can be regarded as reliable has been the subject of American investigation. Research in the US Air Force by Christal, Madden and Harding (1960) suggests that the reliability of results reaches a maximum when between ten and fifteen raters are employed. Taking a simple average of the ratings, the results were at their most reliable, both as between different raters and as between two ratings given by the same person at different points in time, when such a number of assessors was employed. This agrees with Satter (1949) using paired comparisons. In this study two groups of assessors (numbering ten and thirteen respectively), and each composed of both operatives and supervisors, rated jobs against four factors (educational skills, work skills, application skills, and social and personal skills) and produced a higher degree of reliability than when fewer numbers of raters were used. There is not much hard data on reliability co-efficients from very large groups of raters, which in any case tend to be avoided except in the case of computer based techniques. Administratively and politically it is easier to pool ratings to obtain averages than it is to reach consensus. Paired comparisons may be disproportionately time-consuming.

By whatever method, job evaluation is based on comparison—comparison with other jobs, comparison against a 'standard', or by comparing the amount of a factor present in a given set of jobs. Comparative judgements are part of its philosophy. The judgemental process, fallible and vulnerable, is concerned with an interpretation of the stimulus and the selection of appropriate responses inherent or called for in the system. The initial stimulus is the information provided about the job. The job description, or job information sheet, constitutes the fundamental starting point. Any error or bias in the choice and presentation of factual evidence at this stage will be compounded later on, affecting reliability (and more particularly validity) of the whole thing. In practice, when job descriptions are being established, various standards may be applied. Several people in the organisation may have a hand in drafting the final statement. All too often job descriptions turn out to be collections of personnel factors such as education, experience and so on, without any real assessment of the job itself. A job description which is ideally suited for drawing up a job specification for personnel selection is not necessarily the one most suited to job evaluation. The purpose of the description must be borne in mind when facts about the job are assembled and recorded. There is considerable potential for misunderstanding. As Rosemary Stewart (1967) has observed, job descriptions may be statements 'either of what is supposed to happen, or what those think happens, not necessarily what does happen'. The US Air Force studies (Christal, *et al.*) showed that longer, more detailed descriptions tended to inflate assessments, but more important, that provided descriptions were of *uniform* length and detail ratings were consistent. The amount of detail required is less in the non-analytical methods, but whatever type of scheme is adopted, more accurate results are obtained by using descriptions of identical depth and breadth of

123

information, layout and presentation. One of the most frequent criticisms that one hears about job descriptions is that they refer at best to a static situation; that they do not account for job changes over time. This is perfectly true, but not really the problem we have to consider. If the job changes, then it becomes due for re-evaluation, and not only the job analysis, but the whole process of assessment and pricing must be gone through again. We have suggested some hints for job analysis and criteria for making assessments in Chapter 3, but inevitably there are bound to be some variations in emphasis and interpretation. We can do no more than make an effort to minimise the scope of maljudgement.

The actual factors selected for a job evaluation scheme, as well as the format and content of job descriptions, form part of the stimulus and elicit response. Judgements may be affected by the way in which they are structured and weighted. Indeed, the initial weightings themselves being almost arbitrary in their derivation must affect the validity of the scheme. Research in this area is limited, but there are at least a few studies which throw some light on the subject. The classic American studies by Lawshe et al. (1944, 1945, 1946) showed that the same results can be obtained by the use of a simplified system involving fewer characteristics to be rated, a finding supported by Chesler (1948) that the shorter the scale used the better. Lawshe examined which single factor, which two factors, which three factors and so on gave points ratings that correlated highest with total points rating. Amongst hourly paid jobs in three plants, he found that 'experience' (or learning time) was the most important single factor in determining the total points evaluated; the next most important factors were 'hazards' and 'initiative'. The evidence suggests that where factors are used for the evaluation of manual-type jobs, the factors are of differential importance. If one then weights the factors accordingly, one simply maintains *status quo* attitudes about the relative differences between jobs, and the evaluations come out in conformity. Similarly, Hazewinkel (1969) has insinuated that preconceived ideas about the nature of jobs influence the choice of factors, their weightings and subsequent scorings. In jobs demanding intellectual qualities, these factors tend to be specified as 'schooling', 'education', 'experience', 'training', 'initiative' and the like, which he remarks are 'surprisingly similar to what psychologists would call "general intelligence" ' and that 'it is not unusual to find . . .

124

that some combination of these "intellectual requirement factors" will explain more than 90 per cent of the variance of the total score. In such a situation, the addition of factor scores unrelated to the general factor has no influence at all.' This may be true, in which case the only sensible strategy to adopt is to eschew the remaining subsidiary factors and compare jobs against what is effectively a single-factor job evaluation plan. If acceptable ratings could be achieved, not very much, in theory, will have been lost. However, there is the suspicion that this sweeping condemnation (based on opinion, not empirical evidence) advances the cause of simplicity a little too far. The real value of a composite factor range is to facilitate the fine discrimination between jobs in larger-scale enterprise which might be called for where there are differences not only in cognitive inputs, but also in working conditions, levels of responsibility, in the physical and social environment and so on. The crunch issue here has been clearly nailed by Otis and Leukart (1954) who point out that if one is aiming at factor reductions, it is imperative first to use a wider factor range with all the jobs in the survey, and then by statistical analysis to identify those specific factors which would work best for that specific work situation. The pursuit of a shorter factor range is not necessarily *reductio ad absurdam*. The converse of the situation is that by having too many factors, a state of overlapping of factors (co-variance) is very likely to arise, which although perhaps not invalidating the scheme (assuming they have been properly selected) unfortunately does provide an open invitation for a bit more bias and error to creep into assessments, thereby reducing conspect reliability between raters. The problem is to find factors which are criterion related, that is factors genuinely related to the content of jobs in question and which seek to distil out the essential differences between jobs. A textbook example is likely to be invalid. Factor plans must be tailor-made to the work situation. Here, yet again, is another reason why it is almost impossible to have a masterplan relevant to the entire organisation, and why job families should be treated separately. It is on these grounds that something can be said for the all-embracing techniques of Jaques and Paterson which at least attempt to apply universal criteria.

In an age when there is a movement towards quantification in management, one is reminded of the influence of physical scientists, for instance Galileo (1564–1642):

> Count what is countable,
> Measure what is measurable,
> And what is not measurable,
> Make measurable . . .

or Lord Kelvin (1824–1907): 'When you can measure what you are speaking of and express it in numbers, you know that on which you are discoursing. But if you cannot measure it and express it in numbers, your knowledge is of a very meagre and unsatisfactory kind.' One cannot help but wince at the exponents of a points system who muster this sort of argument in defence or propagation of the quantitative technique. The fact of the matter is that awarding numerical values to bits of a job may well be fallacious. The weightings themselves may derive from a deliberate or subconscious attempt to maintain parity with existing differentials between jobs, but above all, it would be dangerous to assume that essentially subjective assessments of factors, weightings and scorings are made any the more objective merely by the acquisition of numerical values. Objectivity is commendable, but at root it is all a matter of judgement. For this reason, points rating systems may be statistically unreliable and may not even be valid. The methodology of breaking a job down into its component parts also invites criticism. The main point is that the separate job factors are not necessarily additive. Professor T. T. Paterson (1972) says it is like adding bananas, oranges, lemons, apples in order to arrive at the total collection of fruit and then making comparisons between the various collections in terms of the total number in each collection. There is quite a lot of truth in this. But the counter argument is that the whole purpose of the points system is to arrive at a summation of the various elements in a job with a view to forming some pragmatic basis on which to make comparison, and if bananas are considered more important than oranges, they must be weighted and scored accordingly. Unless one resorts to a single-factor system, whole-job ranking, decision banding, time-span or whatever, there is no other way of doing it, and there is considerable resistance amongst unions and employees to single-factor rating schemes. The inescapable conclusion is that man's attempts to structure and control the working environment in this way are less than perfect. A balance must be struck between the relative advantages and disadvantages, and one should be aware of where the potential sources of

126

invalidity and unreliability lie. A general observation would be that most firms using points systems seem to be satisfied, on the whole. As a technique it is certainly manageable, understandable (usually), adaptable to changing technological and occupational conditions and can be manipulated politically to achieve whatever the respective parties want. Properly administered it is based on consensus. However, we cannot go completely along with Professor G. F. Thomason (1968) and say that 'the points rating system becomes a clearer part of the portfolio of scientific management, and carries its own connotations of rationality and objectivity or impersonality', although we might feel inclined to go some of the way if we are comparing it with other conventional methods.

Factor comparison comes to mind as a case in point. The delimitation of factors is intended to eliminate covariance, but we should not lose sight of what it is exactly we are trying to measure, and this makes the selection of factors absolutely critical. Factors must be related to the task and skill contents of the job, and any one factor-plan is only likely to be relevant to the job family for which it is intended. The necessity of reproducing a series of factor-plans clearly undermines its practical utility. Again, the criterion of a current wage-rate may be quite invalid. Factor comparison is simply a system designed to fit and support the existing or predetermined rate. The cross-reference between factor rankings and factor evaluations on the face of it provides a cross-check for reliability in two sets of assessments, but in practice with a large number of jobs, the two sets of ratings may be quite unreconcilable without a good bit of juggling to make the two sets of figures achieve the desired correlation. Although a higher degree of reliability is generally claimed for it than whole-job ranking, in the experience of the author, the concentration on just a few factors lends itself to distortion from halo effect.

The non-analytical methods are quicker and cheaper to apply, but they do not draw out the truly significant differences between jobs. They are more subjective. There are no guide lines in ranking, for example, to channel the thought-processes of assessors along the right or even the same lines. Certain arbitrary decisions have to be made, such as where to draw the line between grades. It may be difficult to justify some of these decisions, and contentions about them can lead to wage or salary drift, upward movements in pay to compensate for what may be merely minor accretions to levels of work and responsibility. Unsubstantiated

127

decisions on which ranking is based are an invitation to processes of leap-frogging. Sometimes, too, it is almost invidious to make comparisons between unlike jobs. Paterson's bananas and oranges syndrome again applies. One can really only compare like with like. As Livernash (1954) has observed: 'Jobs within skill families are more closely knit on logical grounds than are job comparisons cutting across such families.' Classification systems obviate the problem of where to draw grade lines, since they are predetermined in accordance with organisational structure, but the subjectivity of job assessment remains. Nor is there any reason to suppose that the criteria for predetermined grades were the right ones.

When all is said and done one may well wonder what is the best policy. On balance, since we live in a world of imperfection, does it really matter which technique is applied? Perhaps not. There is really very little evidence comparing the results of various schemes. The comparisons made internally by individual firms are rarely published, and in any case the 'best' scheme is the one which produces the 'best' result, another subjective assessment. As a matter of interest, we can allude to those comparisons which have been published. Satter (1949) compared the psychological technique of paired comparisons with the job evaluation technique of points rating and found the two methods yielded very similar results. In the UK, whilst a grading scheme was adopted by the National Coal Board on the grounds of its simplicity, the results conformed substantially with those produced in an independent evaluation by Sales and Davies (1957) using points rating. Earlier, Chesler (1948) had already discovered that different schemes produced essentially the same results. This could mean that all the schemes were equally valid, but could just as well mean that each scheme was loaded to produce the desired result. We cannot really say that any one scheme is better than another.

Much of the discussion about theoretical aspects has focused on questions affecting reliability, because these are the deficiencies which are easiest to identify. Central to the whole theme, however, are matters affecting validity. Validity is concerned with the accuracy of job evaluation as an instrument of measurement. Does it in fact measure differentials in a balanced series of jobs? To what extent, if at all, does it measure something else, either hidden or observable? To what extent may it fail to measure certain parts of the problem? Clearly, where degrees of contamination or deficiency exist, the instrument is less than perfectly valid. The messy realities of organisational life, the host of variables controllable and uncontrollable which affect any given situation, sometimes mean that we must make do with a system which is less than perfect simply because we can do no better. However, we should be aware of the imperfections. To answer the question, is job evaluation a valid instrument? one must first specify what it is one is trying to measure. There could in reality be several answers. One could be that we are trying to measure the relative worth of jobs. Another could be that we are trying to arrive at a socially equitable distribution of income. Another, that we seek to determine a fair rate of pay for work done. Precisely because job evaluation can mean different things in different situations and can have varying objectives, the question cannot be answered in general terms. We must be specific about the criterion we are aiming at, what we are trying to achieve. Only then can we seriously think about answering the question. Answers are elusive, for we soon get caught up in circular arguments. One of the easiest ways to validate a technique of job evaluation is to compare its outcome with that of another technique. If the results are compatible, this may demonstrate validity, but conversely it may not; it may simply replicate the faults of the first technique and demonstrate no more than tautology. Another method would be to compare the results of a job evaluation exercise with existing rates. A near-perfect correlation might suggest a high degree of validity, but not necessarily, for the criterion of existing rates may not be the right one. In fact if the criterion of existing or market rates is adopted, one is bound to end up by underwriting the *status quo*. Almost every technique, except perhaps that of Jaques, falls into this trap. Conventional assessments of job worth and the distribution of income are replicated and perpetuated, for which job evaluation seeks to provide rational explanation. In the words of Baroness Wootton (1955), job evaluation 'respects in practice the boundaries set by convention to which in theory it might offer serious challenge'. Perhaps job evaluation is a myth, a mystique for covering up inequities in the social system. What is more, the introduction of a formal system may rigidify and impede the processes of change. The problem enters the political arena. There can be no doubt that the validation of job evaluation of plans as wholes, or the various supposedly correlated factors included in them, is a tricky exercise.

129

Scientifically we would ideally want to show that one approach or method is more valid than another in differentiating between jobs for the purpose of operating a payment system. But we have tended to take the narrow view that this is the sole purpose of job evaluation; we have tended to ignore problems of increasing job satisfaction and performance. If the introduction of job evaluation results in increased job satisfaction as reflected in people's satisfaction with pay and the method by which it is determined, and as evidenced by fewer stoppages, reduced labour turnover, etc., attributable to this factor, then in a sense validity is demonstrated. One measure of validity is whether the system achieves the sort of pay structure people are prepared to accept as just and fair. One of the less commonly extolled virtues of job evaluation, properly instituted, is that it can offer a formula around which consensus can be reached in a given situation.

Although it is difficult to demonstrate validity, although error and bias may creep into the establishment of criteria or into the rating procedures, the methods provide tools of analysis without which decisions about pay would be even more haphazard. Job evaluation can provide a means for correcting existing inequities and guard against the creation of new ones. It provides form and administrative structure. It attempts to apply conventional logic to internal differentials, although its relationship to general levels of wages and salaries is much less clear. Partly this is because the concept of the market rate is yet another myth. 'Market comparisons are rarely possible for a very high proportion of jobs and, where possible, usually yield a fairly wide range of rates frequently with no clear mode' (Livernash, 1954). There is also the difference between the prevailing rate, where it can be established, and the 'buying-in' rate which is usually higher. Job evaluation can only form part of a pay policy.

Apart from the allowances which must be made for merit, seniority and career progression, there is also the inherent danger that any pay policy, however formulated, tends over time gradually and imperceptibly to lose its relevance to the situation for which it was designed, and therefore its validity. The essence of the thing is judgement according to conventional criteria, and inevitably the processes are subjective. The price of a job is much like the price of anything else, a subjective evaluation of what a willing buyer is prepared to pay and a willing seller accept. It is important to take a balanced view of the theoretical issues,

130

for we should beware the pitfalls of uncritical empiricism on the one hand, but equally, of theoretical abstraction on the other.

Chapter 8

Practical Applications

The most extensive survey of the coverage and usage of job evaluation in the UK was that recently carried out by the National Board for Prices and Incomes (NBPI Report 83, 1968), which sampled 8,000 organisations in mining, manufacturing, construction, transport, certain service industries and public utilities. The findings were that mainly large-scale organisations, as measured in terms of payroll strength, use job evaluation to a significant extent. Firms employing more than 5,000 workers were found to apply job evaluation to some 40 per cent of their jobs. Firms employing less than 500 workers applied it on average only to 6 per cent. The survey studied a total of 6,500 jobs. Of these, only 25 per cent were evaluated. They were concentrated in 10 per cent of the establishments. Generally speaking, industries which are dominated by a small number of large firms are those in which job evaluation has made its greatest advance. The trend is true of both private and public sectors of the economy. For example, both in coal mining, a government controlled monopoly, and in the tobacco industry, featured by a high degree of oligopoly, job evaluation is applied to 70 per cent of jobs. Process industries and transport tend also to be oligopolistic. In the oil refining and chemical industries, for instance, 50 per cent of jobs are evaluated, and in air transport, 40 per cent. In industries where there exists freer competition for products and resources, including labour, one finds far less extensive use of job evaluation. Many industries—timber and furniture, textiles, agriculture, fishing, leather and fur, for example—have job relationships deeply rooted in tradition, and here job evaluation has made its least impact. Where minimum wage legislation applies, again one finds little usage. The atmosphere and recent history of industrial relations also seems to be a major influence. Industries which in post-war years have suffered from recurrent labour relations problems—engineering, construction, printing and publishing, shipbuilding—use job evaluation the least. Although these are industries which employ a large number of craftsmen, which could account for the low incidence of job evaluation, the main reason for its not being introduced may well be the absence of good employer-employee relations.

Of various schemes in operation in the UK, the NBPI survey found that 47 per cent were of the points rating type, 28 per cent classification, 20 per cent ranking and 5 per cent factor comparison. Factor comparison is the most piece-meal and time-consuming method to use for a large number of jobs, which may account for its relatively limited use. A more significant observation is that the widespread application of the non-quantitative methods (48 per cent of the total) tends to belie the criticism that their use must be confined to small firms or to a narrow range of jobs. British management may also have a proclivity to shy away from quantification. In terms of categories of jobs evaluated by any method, the coverage was found to be 30 per cent for managerial jobs, 27 per cent for other white-collar jobs, 26 per cent for manual workers and 11 per cent for craftsmen. Most firms apply different schemes for manual workers, staff and managerial employees. The NBPI found virtually no cases of the same scheme being applied to both blue-collar and white-collar jobs. This is no doubt mainly because, as has been explained previously, different factors are involved in the two types of work. The degree of capitalisation and concentration in an industry appears also to have a bearing—it may even dictate the type of job to which evaluation can be applied. For example, in the air transport industry a proportionately larger number of white-collar jobs are evaluated, whereas the reverse is true of the tobacco industry.

By contrast with the US, job evaluation in the UK is still in its infancy. It is largely a post-war, or even post-1950s phenomenon, rapidly gathering momentum. There seems to be a link between the size of the enterprise and the use of job evaluation. The current propensity for organisations to increase in size, due not only to growth, but also to amalgamations and takeovers, is creating new payment problems. Large organisations find problems of cost control exaggerated when faced with a complexity of rates, special allowances and other variations in the pay structure. Simplification is an aid to control. Management

133

seeks efficiency, and job evaluation provides a means to that end. Whilst it is true that current trends and fashion may have some influence, the choice of any particular method will depend on prevailing circumstances —labour intensity of the firm, organisation, expansion, cost structure, type of labour employed and conditions in the local labour market. Management's main objectives are financial control and cost reduction. The experience of most companies is that a net saving can be achieved through simplification of the payment structure and a reduction in the time spent on negotiation. Management's attitude, on these grounds, tends to favour job evaluation. But a price must be paid. Impact costs are bound to arise from its introduction and maintenance. The NBPI (Report 83, 1968) found that resultant increases in payroll costs ranged from 2 per cent to 12 per cent. These were partially accounted for by the fact that the majority of firms in the survey introduced job evaluation as part of a productivity agreement, making it difficult to isolate costs incurred in introducing job evaluation from the overall increase in costs.

Frequently job evaluation is introduced as part of a revision of the wage/salary structure anyway, and some upward movement is to be expected. Job evaluation would be quite unacceptable if it were to result in a depression of payment levels. We are speaking here in general terms. Although it is obvious that individual anomalies above and below par must be adjusted, these are likely to be isolated instances and are unlikely in themselves to affect overall levels. There sometimes exists the sneaking suspicion that the impact of job evaluation is inflationary, but this is a hypothesis which it is difficult to substantiate, particularly where it simply forms part of a reappraisal or reorganisation, and where it primarily acts as an aid to rationalisation. In any case, job evaluation is concerned with basic rates for jobs, and not with premium payments and other additions to pay which may be negotiated separately. Total earnings may be only in part determined by job evaluation methods. Pragmatically, of course, organisations are not likely to introduce or augment job evaluation systems if the results diverge markedly from the existing structure or from market rates, for they would then be likely to suffer labour turnover and recruitment problems were the rates too low, or alternatively, in the opposite situation, face higher costs than their competitors. The NBPI took the view that 'benefits over time should more than outweigh costs' and felt 'disposed to favour' job evaluation, although it did little to encourage its application in practice, mainly because of its own preoccupation with absolutes, rather than with differentials.

The advantages of job evaluation may extend beyond the frontiers of an individual firm. In some cases, job evaluation may, with benefit, be extended to a whole industry. It may even be applied on a national scale. Evidence of this wider use comes from Sweden, the US, Germany, Holland and the USSR. In the UK job evaluation on an industry-wide basis is confined at present to four main industries. Coal mining, under the aegis of the National Coal Board, provides a classic example. Prior to 1955, there existed some 6,500 jobs throughout the industry, and a complex system of rates determined at colliery or local levels by a variety of methods. Many anomalies in pay were felt to exist between jobs of the same content, often within the same colliery. With union participation, the number of jobs was reduced to 400. These were classified into 13 grades for three broad occupational groups: craftsmen (3 grades), underground workers (5 grades), surface workers (5 grades) (Sales and Davies, 1957), and apart from minor modifications, the scheme remains in operation today. A nationalised industry clearly lends itself to industry-wide job evaluation. However, private firms have also on occasion collaborated, through their respective trade associations, with the same objective in view. The main examples are to be found where industries are small in terms of numbers employed, and where they tend to be localised. The jute industry introduced a points rating scheme in 1952, based on an agreement between member companies of the Jute Association. The idea emanated from the findings of the report of the Government's Jute Working Party (1948). As in the case of coal mining, a confused system of pay had arisen, exacerbated by changes in production methods and redeployment of labour. Whilst member companies were never obliged to adopt the system, the majority of firms continue to give their active support. The scheme was further revised and streamlined in 1967 to take account of revised job requirements. A similar situation is to be found in the cotton spinning and doubling industry. Installation of modern machinery, and anomalies in pay based on district wage bargaining, gave impetus to the formation in 1964 of a system which has since been applied to all spinning mills. Employees and unions negotiated an agreement based on a points rating scheme. Associated pay levels were determined by reference to an earlier

135

district wage settlement, and in order to take account of variations in work at plant level, a wage band for each grade was established.

In the US, industry-wide schemes are more highly developed. This is perhaps not surprising in a country where two-thirds of the labour force are under job evaluation of some kind. The first industry-wide schemes were the points adopted by NEMA (National Electrical Manufacturers Association) and its offspring, the NMTA (National Metal Trades Association) scheme (Kress, 1939), and later the US steel scheme, which arose out of the wartime intervention of the National War Labor Board (Stieber, 1959). All these schemes offer broad guidelines for the evaluation of jobs within their respective industries, and interpretation at local level need not be rigid.

In Sweden job evaluation has been directed primarily at the industry level. Systematic job evaluation began after the war with the introduction of industry-wide schemes. There are at present six major schemes (for brewing, paper and pulp, engineering, iron and steel, saw milling and 'general' industries). Experts are available centrally to advise local managements and union representatives. In Swedish industrial relations, unlike British experience, the industry level has always dominated over the local level. Such sweeping introductions of job evaluation are therefore not out of character. Most schemes are of the points rating type, and concentrate on manual workers.

In Germany an interesting situation is to be found in the engineering industry. Collective bargaining in Western Germany is generally conducted on a regional basis, and statutory works councils are responsible for overseeing the implementation of agreements at plant level. The engineering industry is universally heterogeneous in its range of activities. This fact clearly poses problems when it comes to rationalisation. However, in Germany six regional job evaluation schemes have developed from union-management negotiations, mostly based on points rating or factor comparison, and may voluntarily be adopted by firms at the discretion of the works council. In other industries, maybe surprisingly, job evaluation is not necessarily formalised. The chemical industry—and particularly the man-made fibre industry—is reported to have (privately published) well-developed schemes.

If job evaluation can be applied successfully at industry level, there exists by implication the possibility of its application at national level. The reasons for its logical extension may derive from doctrinaire socialism, or in a free market, it may be seen as a useful adjunct to an incomes policy. The Netherlands Government, in 1945, in an attempt to control wage inflation, imposed a wage structure on all manual workers. Manual jobs were divided into the three categories of 'skilled', 'semi-skilled', and 'unskilled' in accordance with the traditional notions of worker differentiation. A fixed percentage differential was applied to the wages for the three grades, and a regional cost-of-living allowance was superimposed. Continuing inflationary pressures necessitated a wage freeze in 1946. Increases in wages were then permitted only where they resulted from the introduction of job evaluation methods in an attempt to rationalise wage structures (Zoeteweij, 1955). Consequently, job evaluation spread rapidly. Not surprisingly, a number of spurious job evaluation schemes emerged in an effort to substantiate wage claims. The objectives were undermined. As a result the Government was obliged to establish a national committee for the purpose of devising a single scheme for uniform application thoughout industry. The method finally selected was a ten factor points rating scheme, termed the 'Standardisation Method', based on two extreme key jobs—at one end of the scale, the work of the unskilled labourer—and at the other, the work of the skilled engineering mechanic. Wage increases were not granted unless they could be substantiated through this particular scheme. A national graduated scale of payment was introduced, which ensured that jobs achieving the same points score held the same basic pay. Differentials were set in relation to the two extreme grades.

The Dutch attempt at national job evaluation was at the same time an attempt both to contain wage inflation and to establish equitable differential levels of payment. For a time the policy succeeded. Cost-push inflation was dampened, but with the disappearance of the symptoms of the malady, there arose considerable opposition, from employers and unions, to the rigidity imposed by central control (Celtinger, 1964). By the late 1950s opposition was so great that the Government was forced to abandon the scheme in its original form. In principle, centralised job evaluation is still very active, although it is less tightly controlled. Currently, some 70 per cent of manual workers' wages are determined in this way. Dutch experience suggests, however, that the application of a national job evaluation scheme, whatever its merits in theory, is far from easy. In the first place it is difficult in a democratic society to gain acceptance of centralised control. In the

137

second place it is extremely difficult to devise an evaluation scheme which is sufficiently comprehensive to encompass the wide spectrum of skills, aptitudes and efforts demanded of a complete range of economic activities.

The USSR seems to have been more successful. Since all workers are state employees, wages, certainly since the war, have been a matter of public policy. The State Committee publishes job descriptions, allocates jobs to appropriate grades and determines wage differentials. For many years the only jobs considered suitable for job evaluation, as such, were those of narrow structural range and limited intellectual content. Only manual and low-level clerical jobs were evaluated. Higher, especially executive jobs, were awarded income levels by much more arbitrary means. Since 1964, combined research in socialist countries (Kordaszewski, 1969) has produced principles for job evaluation which are now being applied to manual and non-manual workers throughout the USSR. The Soviet scheme, so far as can be ascertained, formed part of a major overhaul of the national incomes structure, to meet economic and social objectives, and to encourage internal mobility of labour.

For Britain, a move in the Dutch direction would impose an unpopular if not intolerable intervention in traditional collective bargaining procedures, although in contemporary debate about incomes policy the question of a national job evaluation scheme has been raised. The assumptions are that universal criteria can be found (Brown, 1973) and that it is possible to come to grips with the *earnings-gap*, i.e. the difference between basic rates and total emoluments, a gap which has been generally widening since the last war through the pressure of local bargaining groups who have succeeded in gaining various additions and allowances of one kind or another superimposed on the basic rate. Job evaluation, certainly in its conventional forms, is concerned with the basic rate for the job, yet an incomes policy, to be successful, must concern itself with total earnings, and further with the seemingly unreconcilable problem of variations in earnings as between occupations and industries and the demonstrable preoccupation of vested interests to maintain such differentials (Clegg, 1971). Incomes policy faces the twin problems of absolutes and relativities. Job evaluation really only gives a guide towards internal consistency with regard to relativity, or at best, on a fairly narrow or local front, to relativities between strictly comparable occupations. Where, as obtains in the UK at the moment, existing pay structures are highly heterogeneous and far from equitable or egalitarian, the contribution of job evaluation in its present form of sophistication is exceedingly limited on a national front. Whether the techniques could be further refined to extend their applicability is doubtful, hence the search for common, as opposed to specific, norms and criteria of general validity (Jaques, Paterson, etc.).

Institutional factors are also important. In the case of Sweden, for example, a tighter measure of control is possible than could currently obtain in Britain, because of the existence of central negotiations and highly centralised organisations of workers and employers. This is not to argue a case in favour of a move in the Swedish direction, but simply to point out cultural differences and underline the necessity for a unique, individual approach. Institutional factors apart, however, job evaluation at any level must be related to the organisational climate and conditions within an industry if it is to be successful. A potential source of enmity could well exist between the edicts of a centralised system—be it at firm, industry or national level—and the flexibility required to make it acceptable and applicable at the grass roots.

One benefit accredited to job evaluation, which needs treating with some reservation, is that by introducing a systematic approach much of the friction of wage negotiations is avoided. An objective of employees is to maximise pay, and that of management is to minimise cost. A conflict of interests exists from the outset. The problem remains whether job evaluation is applied or not. The outcome of wage negotiations at firm or shop floor level depends on the resolution of conflict through bargaining channels. Compromise has to be reached on the extent of benefit received by either party.

The Trades Union Congress has not issued a policy statement on the general acceptability of job evaluation which, as in most matters of policy, it regards as the prerogative of the individual union, but it has concerned itself to ensure that systems do not preclude joint negotiation (TUC, 1969). British unions expect the initiative to come from management, but are fearful of its arbitrary imposition. Unions have a number of specific contentions. Subjectivity comes under fire. Unions are apprehensive about subjective judgements; they fear that job descriptions, weightings and points allocations may be inaccurately assessed. The TUC has made this point forcibly. However, the criticism that job evaluation is subjective, although it may be regarded as valid, applies equally, of course, to negotiation. Another point is that unions are anxious not to confuse the rate for the job with the rate for the ability to do the job—a different factor, and one more appropriate for merit rating than payment by results. This is precisely how the disputation over craftsmen has arisen. Attempts to apply job evaluation to craft jobs have met with limited success. The attitude of craft unions has always been that their members should be regarded as warranting special treatment because of the skills they bring to the job.

The question of differentials is the most vexed of all. Unions contend that wage levels and differential payments result from the interaction of a number of factors, and that it is difficult to identify, isolate and measure their individual effects. It is felt that job evaluation may impose a degree of restriction on existing negotiating arrangements, for it examines only those factors limited to the content of the job, and the requirements of the firm or industry. The approach is regarded as too narrow, for it does not take sufficient account of external influences. Gomberg (1951) for instance, regards job evaluation from the trade unionist's point of view as merely a subordinate tool to collective bargaining. A fierce attack once came from the International Association of Machinists of the USA (1954) with the claim that job evaluation creates an obstacle to the correction of inequities, and fails to consider the influences of supply and demand, or regional differences in the labour market. This is perhaps rather sweeping, and unlikely to obtain in a competitive firm. The Association further claimed that the individual is ignored, as regards his ability, loyalty, length of service, and that a barrier is created between worker and job because the method of determining the relative worth of the job is not understood by the employee. Above all, a ceiling is imposed on wages which is contrary to the traditional aim of organised labour to negotiate pay increases. The view is held that job evaluation undermines the standing of unions, since it encourages workers to argue against each other rather than with management. Whilst it is true that the technique might be applied in an arbitrary fashion, or as a defence mechanism against unions on pay issues, it must equally be accepted that job evaluation, like any other technique, must depend for its success on the manner in which it is employed.

Despite the criticisms which have been made, job evaluation schemes have been installed with the co-operation of trade unions in the UK and

140

abroad, and have been successful in producing more acceptable pay structures. Unions recognise that job evaluation provides a systematic approach to analysing jobs and draws attention to anomalies. The system must be formalised. To the extent that an agreed framework can be devised from liaison between management and worker representatives, arbitrary decisions can be minimised, and complaints that management does not give sufficient information can be mitigated.

Chapter 9

Salary Administration and Job Evaluation

This chapter is devoted to salaries rather than to wages. Wage administration forms a concise area and is already well documented, but salary administration tends to remain a loose collection of factors. More particularly, job evaluation has made its greatest impact in the salaries sector. As cited previously, the NBPI (Report No. 83, 1968) found that 'the highest coverage occurs in the "managerial" category, where 30 per cent of the group is covered, followed by "staff", with 27 per cent'.

Salary administration is that broad area of personnel management which refers to the determination of appropriate levels of remuneration for staff employees according to the grade or worth of the job, coupled with a consideration of individual merit and performance and tempered by company profitability. It does not refer to the actual mechanisms of payment or the running of the payroll; this is usually a financial or accounting function.

On the face of it, salary payment systems are relatively straightforward as compared to wage payment systems, at least in so far as their compilation is concerned. The amounts paid are determined on an annual basis and divided normally into twelve equal monthly instalments (or maybe appropriate weekly instalments). Bonuses, commission, fringe benefits, might be superimposed, but are usually regarded as separate items. For salaries, payment is at flat rate, and theoretically includes the rate for the job plus a reward for performance or service. Frequently the performance element is rather vague. Sometimes the whole of the salary structure is secret. Rarely does one find a comprehensive salary policy in which all things are set out precisely. Conventional wisdom in this field is not particularly helpful and theoretical foundation is lacking.

142

Considering the importance of salaried staff to the success of an enterprise, the rather nebulous and haphazard orthodoxy, such as it is, is rather surprising. By salaried staff we include the whole of the managerial echelon, plus clerical, technical, professional and sales staff, and nowadays, manual workers who have been accorded 'staff status' in a number of leading organisations. On the whole, salary administration is a sadly neglected area of personnel management, one which lacks intellectual stimulation. Consequently research evidence is sparse. One of the few serious pieces of investigation was another piece of work carried out by the NBPI (Report No. 132, 1968) which made some telling observations:

'The increasing importance of salaries as a component of the total earned incomes is not always realised. In 1968 salaries accounted for 35 per cent of all employment incomes in manufacturing industries, whereas the proportion ten years earlier was 29 per cent. . . . This increase in importance is in itself justification for a growing interest in the principles on which salary systems are based. There are, in addition, specific pressures which are likely to lead to increasing rationalisation. These include: greater awareness of opportunities on the part of salary earners themselves, itself a concomitant of rising educational levels, higher expectation, greater mobility and a proliferation of specialised skills; the trend towards larger industrial units through growth, mergers and takeovers; the activities of management selection firms; and the increasing extent to which the work and interest of white-collar unions have affected the actions of management and have come to the attention of salaried staff. All these factors are also likely to bring about a greater interest in recognisable and logical systems and structures, and to lead away from salaries determined, usually in secret, on a purely personal *ad hoc* basis.'

The trends noted in the report have continued to operate. Salaries probably now account for nearer 40 per cent of employment incomes, and it may well be that white-collar salary earners will actually outnumber hourly paid manual wage earners by the 1980s. It is therefore timely to consider the issues involved. The cost of salaries to the employing organisation, already large, is an increasing element of the total payroll budget. Certain techniques contributing towards a salary administration policy have been with us for some years. The chief of these

143

are job evaluation, performance appraisal and review systems, career progression policies, salary budgeting and forward costing. Unfortunately they tend to exist as separate entities. Attempts to co-ordinate them into a unified policy have been piece-meal. Partly this is due to the fact that no one is really quite sure how to go about it, and partly too because the various elements commonly fall within different management functions, notably personnel management and financial management, and tend to remain discrete.

Salary administration itself is not something that can be looked at in isolation. Salary administration is really an attempt to achieve the objectives formulated in a salary policy, which itself, ideally, ought to be a plan, not simply to pay fair and equitable salaries, but to relate and reconcile the career aspirations of employees in terms of current and potential earnings, job satisfaction and personal development to total organisational objectives. In practice a tall order, complicated by the host of variables involved. It is perhaps easier to talk about the problem and to agree to the spirit of the philosophy than to carry it out. Although probably few, if any, organisations can carry it out to the letter, attempts can be made. The aim is really no more than a restatement of the generally accepted principle that manpower policy should be a constituent part of corporate strategy.

Salaries (and wages too) are at the same time both a cost and an investment. Their costs are reflected in the cost of the final product or service. They are an investment in that they represent money spent on a factor or production—labour—in an attempt to earn a dividend. The constituents of salary policy must therefore embrace such crucial factors as the objectives of the organisation, its finances, cash flow and profitability, the state of the labour market, expected demand and supply of various types of labour, government regulations on pay, anticipated expansion or contraction of the organisation, its structure and so forth, as well as the personal aspirations of individuals which have already been mentioned. In so far as the organisation wishes to survive, it will normally be expected to balance its books and make a profit. In such circumstances economic considerations may well assume prime importance. Here one comes to the crux of the problem: 'What is a job of work really worth? What is its economic contribution?'

This is the oldest of chestnuts. According to the tenets of classical economics, the price of labour as a factor of production (wages and salaries) is determined in a free market by the interplay of demand and supply, and the price will obtain where these two forces are in equilibrium. There are assumed to be no shortages in the supply of labour, and further that it is of a homogeneous nature, perfectly mobile and fully aware of all employment opportunities. As regards the demand for labour, this depends on two variables, first the demand for the product to be produced, and secondly upon the productivity of labour itself.

The theory focuses on the margin, the cost and the expected return, of employing one more unit of labour. Marginal productivity theory, as it is called, states that units of labour should be employed up to that point where marginal cost equates with marginal revenue. In other words, the employer calculates that if the contribution to profitability exceeds the cost of taking on labour, it is advantageous to continue to do so up to that point where the cost of employing one more man (marginal cost) is equal to that man's individual contribution (marginal revenue). Thereafter, recruitment should cease, for the firm is in an optimum position. The whole rests on the further assumptions that the objective of the firm is to maximise profits and that perfect competition exists between firms.

Clearly the model is purely abstract and divorced from reality. In real life the market for labour, and competition between firms, is manifestly imperfect, with pronounced tendencies towards oligopoly, monopoly and monopsony. Moreover, how does one calculate marginal productivity? How does one calculate the marginal revenue obtained by hiring one more assistant, clerk, research worker, engineer, accountant or personnel officer? It is just not possible. They are hired because their contribution would seem (often subjectively) to facilitate the work process. Objective measurement is elusive. And of course labour is far from homogeneous. The dehumanised assumption of interchangeable units of labour as a factor of production is a myth. People possess and exercise widely differing skills, capacities and technical specialisms. Economists have been mesmerised by the search for neat models of universal validity, and although classical theory has been refuted, no new acceptable and uncontroversial model has emerged. Economic theory alone does not provide the answers. We are faced with people's differential abilities, attitudes to work and to various management styles, their expectations and preferences, as well as their degrees of combination to bargain terms and conditions of employment, to codify

145

and restrict methods of working and/or exploitation, to withdraw their labour and so on.

In this connection Professor Paterson (1972) has remarked: 'The theories of the economists on the origin and forms of plant wage structures do not hold; it is no wonder that job evaluation has been, for many years, the field of the occupational psychologist.' Gordon McBeath (1969), however, has attempted to compromise the situation, and probably gets quite near the truth, when he says:

'Market value theory [of job value determination] assumes that the economic laws which apply in other commodity markets with variable supply and demand will also apply to the evolution of salary values. In the case of salaries, there are supplies of individuals with widely varying abilities, and demands for wide varieties of people. The supply of and demand for each particular category influence what is currently paid, within constantly evolving patterns of values. . . . These analyses lead to the conclusion that *it is individuals who have market values*. It is through their availability and willingness to do various types of job that job market values emerge, and *it is the combined pattern over hundreds or thousands of people with related skills and abilities which produce the market group*. . . . There is no absolute scale of values, only a constantly changing set of relationships.'

Neither economics nor job evaluation can provide clear and unequivocal predictors of what the rate for the job should be, but what job evaluation can offer is a means for marshalling the various forces together and for interrelating comparable units of work requiring comparable sets of skills and capacities with prevailing market conditions. Beyond this it is difficult to be explicit. What job evaluation *per se* cannot achieve to the satisfaction of a financial planner or corporate strategist is a precise quantification of the value of work being done, partly because of limitations in the techniques, and partly because it is only a partial measurement, namely of the work element itself, and does not include personal merit.

Large, modern organisations seek to budget ahead for all foreseeable cost items, salaries included. A five-year period is frequently chosen, or whatever time period fits in with corporate and manpower plans. In the words of the NBPI report:

'Proper use should be made of salary budgeting as an instrument of control. This has two aspects. First, the budget should be built up on a resource basis—including manpower forecasts—and not simply by assuming that the salary bill will rise by a given percentage. Secondly, actual expenditure should be checked monthly or quarterly against forecast expenditure, and the reasons for major discrepancies investigated.'

The contribution of job evaluation is again limited. It can help to identify the number of people employed within different categories and can identify how the salary budget is apportioned. It forms a framework for administering 'mid-point control'—a technique sometimes adopted for ensuring that total salaries roughly equal the sum of the mid-points of the salary ranges in which all jobs are placed—and for measuring 'attrition'—where average salary levels are reduced if personnel move out of one particular category with cheaper replacements taken on. But these are instruments of salary control which are really quite separate and additional exercises.

There is the further complication that manpower costs tend nowadays to be regarded as fixed rather than variable. It is becoming increasingly difficult, as a result of recent legislation (such as Trade Union and Labour Relations Act, 1974, Contracts of Employment Act, 1963, and Redundancy Payments Act, 1965), to lay off labour of any sort at short notice. The accounting aspects need rethinking.

Traditionally, labour as an economic factor of production, has not been regarded as an asset in the accounting sense. It does not appear on the balance sheet. Social scientists have for some years now argued that business activity which ignores the human factor is likely to lead to non-optimal decisions (Likert, 1967). The ideas of Paton (1932), the first accountant to recognise publicly the value of human assets, were disregarded until quite recently. Largely this has been due to inherent difficulties in quantification. Hekimian and Jones (1967) in a celebrated article resuscitated the issue, and suggested capitalisation of salary as a possible solution. Other ideas quickly followed (Gilbert, 1970), such as replacement costs and acquisition costs. The accountancy profession is moving towards the acceptance of the idea of recording both physical and human assets, and there is contemporary discussion on how to go about it.

A joint study has been made by the Institute of Personnel Management and the Institute of Cost and Management Accountants (Giles and Robinson, 1972). They have formulated a theory of human asset accounting based on the concept of multiplying salaries and wages by factors (human asset multipliers). The factors concerned are those which would normally form part of a conventional job evaluation exercise, for example, qualifications and technical expertise, experience of the job requirements, personal qualities and attitudes, promotion capability, replacement scarcity, loyalty and expectation of future service. The results provide an index of asset value which it is claimed can be checked against the goodwill element of an enterprise valued as a going concern.

'Personnel costs incurred in maintaining or developing the human asset value in a period are grossed up, using the appropriate human asset multipliers. Summaries of changes in the value of the human asset between periods can be produced, highlighting the effects of expenditure on different job grades within the organisation. The theory can be applied quickly and simply to all types of organisation ... [but] is still in an embryonic stage.'

The theory embodies accountancy principles, but some of the assessments are necessarily subjective, such as the judgements relating to various factors. This is analogous, it is argued, to the valuation of a business on a going concern basis.

Clearly any form of human asset accounting has a multitude of facets. There are certain easily quantifiable aspects such as recruitment costs and training costs, others at which quantification can be attempted, such as the value of work currently being done, the value of the skills currently being exercised, and others much more nebulous such as the potential development value of the individuals in an organisation. Job evaluation, which looks at the value of the work and market rates for various skills, can make a significant contribution to measuring the value of human resources employed.

However, it is not only from the point of view of cost control and auditing that salary administration ought to be concerned. There are not only economic factors, but also motivational, organisational and environmental ones. An example of a practical approach to a complex situation is illustrated by some interesting recent work by Professor Tom Lupton and Dan Gowler (1969) of the Manchester Business

School. They draw attention to the wide range of factors which have to be taken into account in selecting a wage payment system. These include product markets, labour markets, technology, and the attitudes and expectations of trade unions and workpeople. They tackle the basic question of 'What combination of organisation, environment and payment system is best fitted to satisfy a given set of objectives?' Although their payment system classification based on a logical grid, being concerned with wages is not really of much help in formulating salary policy decisions, their model does point to two important considerations. The first is that salaries are not—or should not be—determined in isolation from other factors in the system; a decision to increase salaries or alter the salary structure should not be taken without reference to other factors such as recruitment and promotion policy or changes in organisational design or office procedure. The second is that the 'effort-reward' or 'effort bargain' is in fact a complex set of relationships. As Lawler and Porter (see Chapter 2) have indicated, the personal decision to respond or not to respond to financial inducements can be influenced by a number of factors. Therefore a policy decision on salary matters needs to take them into account—not least the perception of the salaried employee as to whether extra effort on his part is likely to result in increased reward or satisfaction. 'Yet how many companies,' writes Camilla McDougall (1973), 'operate standardised across-the-board personnel policies, based apparently on the assumption that the employees concerned are alike in terms of their values and the rewards that they want for their efforts.'

We have seen (in Chapter 2) that man is capable of responding to a myriad of motivators. He seeks to satisfy basic needs, but beyond these will aspire for achievement, recognition, status, esteem, and opportunities for realising his full potential. We have further seen that human behaviour is not uniform. Different individuals may be at different stages of development, aspirations vary, and the role which financial reward can play as a purveyor of certain satisfactions is by no means easy to codify. Moreover, in the business world, financial compensation is not a strict and simple matter of salary. A whole range of fringe benefits, pensions, company cars, expense accounts, profit sharing schemes, share ownership, life and sickness insurance policies, paid holidays, housing and children's education facilities, discounts on company merchandise and so on combine to form the compensation package. Even salary has to be looked at both from the view of current earnings and potential possible earnings, and in turn must be weighted against such considerations as job satisfaction, security, freedom, scope for development and the like.

Insufficient attention generally seems to be paid to how the company's rewards can be distributed in order to achieve the optimum mix of salary and fringe benefits. Cost considerations clearly play a part, as well as tax law, but it may be cheaper, for example, to give a staff employee the use of a company car than, say, an extra £400 or £500 a year in salary, and the individual may well prefer it. Similarly, the up-and-coming executive aged 35 years, with certain domestic commitments and a certain salary, will probably have quite different needs and preferences from the general plant manager or divisional director aged 55 years. A case can be made out for what the Americans call the 'cafeteria' approach, where the employee has freedom to select various bits of the compensation package. Tailoring the reward to suit the individual could well have positive motivational effects. Administratively, the approach is likely to push up costs, and may therefore not be feasible for the entire range of salaried staff. But the point is that the results of a job evaluation exercise do not necessarily have to be paid off in such mechanical manner as so many pounds sterling in straight salary, although they usually are.

Normal practice is to assume that people do work very largely for money. Certainly people seem to expect and look forward to growth in real incomes. Reward systems are designed to compensate for the level of work done—this is where job evaluation plays its part—but in addition, for performance, age, length of service, to retain employees, to provide them with progressive increases in salary over time in line with their career development, to protect them against external inflationary pressures and to pass on to them some of the increases in company profitability. Salaries are made up of a number of strands and a salary policy must take them all into account. Job evaluation can determine the main proportion, but all the rest need to be superimposed in some way. There is plenty of scope for confusion, and very little guidance. There appears to be nowhere, for instance, any clear and unequivocal indication of how much of the salary pay packet should be devoted to the level of work, and how much to merit, performance or any of these other factors. It is largely a matter of discretion or convenience and what has developed as conventional practice within any particular organisation. Worse than that, frequently neither employer nor employee have the slightest idea what it is exactly they are paying for or being paid for. This is motivationally unsettling, and not really conducive to salary control. Whilst it is true that one of the advantages of having a broad group of evaluated jobs falling within a certain fairly broad pay range provides for flexibility in arriving at the actual salary, flexibility without form or laid down lines of policy can only lead to ambiguity and anomaly.

Where such malpractices occur they do not in the least discredit job evaluation, but rather the salary administrators who fall into the trap of thinking that having set up job evaluation the rest of the story will take care of itself. What is needed as an indispensable ingredient for a successful salary policy is a clear decision on the way in which salaries are to be built up. For example, the rate for the job as measured by a job evaluation may account (say) for 80 per cent of the total, performance 10 per cent and length of service 10 per cent. There can then be no quibble about what a man is being paid for, and the man himself will know what the job is worth, how much is due to his own personal efforts, and so on. Preferably such policy decisions should be based on the consensual agreement of management and employees, arrived at in the manner set out in Chapter 3.

A distinction at this stage ought to be drawn, of course, between those organisations which rely heavily on some form of incentive payment (e.g. most manufacturing firms) and those in which increases in salary are a prerogative of length of service (e.g. universities) and where incremental awards are automatic. In any event, the mechanics behind the scheme need to be formalised and publicised. Where incentive payments are concerned, there is the thorny question of the appropriate timing of the salary review and the performance review. Some authorities argue for their separation (Randall, et al, 1972). Where MBO schemes are in operation, it may well be advisable to keep salary review distinct from a review of performance, for where they are combined, the one inevitably tends to cloud the other, probably to the detriment of mutual confidence in target setting and appraisal.

There is the further matter of adding in cost-of-living increases. Some organisations make cost-of-living awards at periodic intervals and keep them separate from merit awards. This is probably the better practice

151

both from the point of view of the employer's own information, and from the point of view of administrative simplicity, since if the awards are made on a percentage basis, the salary brackets for different grades can be moved up accordingly, likewise the points at which people are paid within them, so that relativities remain constant. These constitute general movements in salary, in the same way as when a company decides on an all-round increase due to enhanced profitability, as opposed to individual movements.

Individual movements are related to performance, promotability and the organisation's policy on salary progression. It is sometimes held that salary progression ought to bear some relation also to the number of grades in the system, whether 'broad-banded' (i.e. a few grades) or 'multigrade' (many grades), the spread of range and overlap between grades. This is not necessarily so. Grading structures are largely matters of organisational convenience—this is the prime reason for their being structured in a given way. Salary progression policy is really a separate issue, something superimposed. On the relative advantages of broad-banded various multi-grade structures, the NBPI report concluded that: 'In practice there may be less distinction between the two types of structure than might be thought at first sight. To some extent, the concepts of moving through a single wide grade and moving through a hierarchy of narrow grades can be so applied as to produce very similar effects for the organisation or for the individuals concerned.' Although one could argue a case either way according to personal preference, there appear to be no research findings that support one system rather than another.

It may be helpful to summarise the main points of a salary policy:

1. It should form a constituent and integral part of manpower policy.

2. Salaries should primarily be based on the worth of the job as determined by job evaluation.

3. Job grades facilitate administrative structure, but do not provide the whole story in determining pay.

4. The system should provide scope for rewarding personal merit, performance and length of service.

5. A policy for salary progression should be built in, related to the number of job grades and to the review procedure.

6. The system should be flexible—for instance to facilitate the deployment and internal mobility of staff, and to accommodate changes due to external inflationary pressures and changes in relative market values.

7. The system should help to recruit and retain suitable employees.

8. All parties should be aware of the respective components of the system.

9. It should facilitate costing and control.

10. The situation is never static, and a constant assessment should be made of the future, with regard to forecasts and budgets.

If nothing else, it is surely apparent that questions of salary administration are wide-ranging and far-reaching. Consensus about any 'best' system is lacking, and the factors concerned tend not to be integrated. There is a body of knowledge available, but it does not form a unified whole. Salary administrators are clearly faced with a plethora of problems and no easily defined, clear-cut solutions. One is reminded of lines from W. H. Auden (1907–73):

> The last word on how we may live or die
>   Rests today with such quiet
> Men, working too hard in rooms that are too big
>   Reducing to figures
> What is the matter, what is to be done.

Chapter 10

Summary and Conclusion

SUMMARY

Debate centres around the relative importance of money as a reward for work. No firm conclusion is possible. At least money must be regarded as a 'maintenance' factor, and for that reason alone the rate for the job must be got right. Depending on the individual's perception, pay can be seen as a reward or recognition for effort and performance and so contribute to personal satisfaction. People are likely to look for a link between effort and reward and for a link between effort and performance. They will seek a state of equilibrium in balancing the two sets of ratios. These processes are highly subjective. Measurement of reward values, effort and performance in quantitative terms is difficult. What matters is an individual's perception of the situation rather than the actuality. Effort is further modified by one's capacities and inclinations and how one sees one's work role in relation to others. Generalisation is not really possible, because of differences between individuals, and because people do not always act logically and rationally in pursuit of their goals.

In the long run the success of any payment system depends on how well it is accepted by the population it serves. What is felt in terms of satisfaction with pay depends in turn on how an individual perceives it as fair and just reward in relation to the effort he has put forth in harnessing his physical, cognitive and conative abilities in order to do the job successfully, and in relation to what he sees other people earning in return for their own skills and efforts.

Job evaluation analyses the human inputs brought to a job and the demands it makes upon the incumbent. It seeks to assemble this information in a logical manner so that comparative decisions can be made between jobs. Its purpose is to arrange for an equitable distribution of available wealth within the constraints of the overriding criteria of company profitability, willingness to pay, prevailing market forces, and the sort of compensation policy an organisation wishes to see emerge. Basic prerequisites for the successful installation of job evaluation are that it should be based on consensual agreement of workpeople concerned, and on a careful, detailed analysis of jobs, recorded in a standard format.

The main conventional methods of job evaluation are based on either a quantitative or a qualitative assessment. Quantitative techniques are the more elaborate, but are capable of producing more discriminating results. Non-quantitative techniques are quicker and easier to apply, and in some cases may be quite acceptable. In either case the techniques determine relative differences between jobs and are not of themselves concerned to establish absolute monetary values. The pricing of the structures which emerge from job evaluation forms a separate, additional exercise.

Recent thinking has suggested that conventional techniques are too subjective and, in addition, simply reflect the relative bargaining powers of the parties engaged in negotiation. Instead, Jaques has suggested measuring the differences between jobs according to the 'time-span of discretion' in the discretionary element of a job, and claims that in this way a general and universal pay structure can be established which is both fair and equitable. He has observed that people have ideas about what constitutes fair pay for work and that these unconsciously held norms for various types and levels of work correlate highly with their respective time-spans. The theory is attractive, but its practicality is highly questionable. Paterson has also taken up the idea of a common yardstick applicable to the evaluation of jobs of all types and levels, using the single factor of 'decision making'. His proposal provides a unitary basis for comparing jobs throughout the employment range, across firms and across industries, but the outcome does little more than reinforce existing pay differentials.

In view of the widespread interest in job evaluation and the sheer size of the scope for implementation in large-scale organisations, a number of management consultancy firms have developed their own systems, available to client companies on a fee-paying basis. These schemes are

155

usually quantitative in character, and are frequently based on variations of the points method.

Any scheme should aim at a high degree of reliability and validity. Reliability refers to consistency of results. Rarely does one find techniques which are perfectly reliable, largely due to error and bias in human judgement. It is helpful, however, to try to identify where sources of imperfection lie, for not until then can any attempts at corrective action be taken. Validity is concerned with the accuracy of job evaluation as an instrument of measurement, a theoretical criterion which it is difficult to demonstrate in practice.

Theoretical considerations apart, the applications of job evaluation in the UK and abroad are widespread. Its usage is increasing. Most advance has been made in the salaried sector; greatest resistance comes from craftsmen. There is evidence to suggest that job evaluation can contribute to rational payment systems on a wider net than just the individual firm. There are examples of industry-wide schemes, and even national ones. Certain lessons can be drawn from the experiences of other countries, such as the problems of centralised control, and finding schemes that are broad enough to encompass a wide range of jobs.

In the area of salary administration, where it is particularly relevant, it can again help towards achieving rational structures, and can help to stabilise, control and forecast manpower costs. It cannot stand in isolation. It can only form part of a pay policy, and must be seen in relation to rewards for seniority and performance and does not of itself solve problems of salary policy, career progression or human asset accounting.

CONCLUSION

To the sceptic, job evaluation may appear as yet another mechanistic technique to regiment the work-force, or to present such a handful of problems as to be not worth the candle. One commentator has remarked: 'Job evaluation may be interpreted as the end to individualism' (Henley, 1972), and more cynically, Tony Cliff (1970): 'Job evaluation and grading are used by managements to reduce workers still further to the status of interchangeable cogs in a machine and at the same time to foster divisions among workers.' There may occasionally be instances where the truth of these allegations can be substantiated. On the whole, the comments are probably extreme. One of the things which has been stressed in this book is the need for co-operation and consensus. Genuine participation, both on the objectives and the methods, should obviate such dire consequences. The fact of the matter is that without job evaluation, or some semblance of structure of one kind or another, anomalies, confusion and unrest are likely to be rampant. While complete *laissez-faire*, or anarchy, may be conducive to the preservation of individualism, it is surely not in the long-run interests of anyone, management or worker, to have a complete Dutch auction in which the strongest will flourish and the weakest flounder. It is all a question of balance, and the way in which job evaluation is implemented.

Of course there are problems. Few things in life are perfect. Job evaluation, with all its imperfections, exists as a major technique for determining pay because it is the best system yet devised which incorporates the concepts of logic, justice and equity, which can be made acceptable to all parties, which incorporates a high degree of flexibility, and which is capable of modification and updating according to changing circumstances. Further, job evaluation can embrace large groups of employees, so that uniformity of treatment on pay matters, and hence fairness, can prevail. If anything, its major weaknesses are more likely to militate against management than against workers, namely in that its implementation tends to be expensive, and usually being introduced by specialists, either from outside the company or from the personnel department, imposes restrictions on the freedom of action and authority of line management. The upward movement in costs is largely due to the golden rule that there should be no pay cuts as the result of job evaluation, and where underpaid jobs are unearthed, their rates should be aligned upwards. It is perhaps not surprising to find that resistance from management levels can be as great an obstacle to installing a scheme as resistance from employees or unions.

In the final analysis, job evaluation does not do very much more than codify market rates for particular levels of skill and responsibility and create a framework for wage/salary control and career progression. As far as market rates are concerned, 'all evaluation of work is a reflection of entrenched social values, rather than an objective statement of truly absolute values. . . . The market therefore imposes its influence on the social pattern and men are paid what it is necessary to pay to get

157

them' (Lyons, 1971). One of the criticisms commonly directed against job evaluation is its asserted propensity to freeze differentials. Since pay levels are determined by the market rather than job evaluation, and not vice versa, the contention is false. In so far as job evaluation can help towards formulating a grading structure, this facilitates career planning, and should act favourably to recruit and retain staff.

Most job evaluation schemes lead to considerable simplification. Salary structures are normally fairly straightforward anyway and the gains of introducing job evaluation, from the point of view of simplification, may not be so great. But many wage payment systems in the UK are sometimes so complicated as to be virtually incomprehensible, and a technique which is capable of reducing a mess to sensible dimensions, without losing relevance to the job of work concerned or reducing real earnings, ought to be welcomed.

Currently attention has been given to proposals for a national job evaluation scheme in Britain. One should be quite clear about what it is intended to achieve. Commonly it is asserted that it will help to control the pace of inflation. If it were true that the inflationary ills of the UK were predominantly due to upward movements of wages and salaries unrelated to increases in productivity, there might be a case for exercising some central control in this way. But there is no real evidence for this. Inflationary pressures are due to a number of factors, including the supply of money, primary product prices and the terms of trade, the exchange rate, the general level of interest rates, fiscal policy, public spending and public borrowing. Although it might be a logical extension from a national incomes policy, with a succession of temporary norms and freezes, to go for national job evaluation, it would not necessarily get to the heart of the matter. Moreover, there would be acute problems of implementation; they might even be insurmountable. Much of the bickering about wage increases revolves around the vexed question of differentials obtaining for different types of work. When one group secures a wage increase, another then wishes to restore its relative position. It is not really conceivable that a national job evaluation plan would be acceptable to all men. On top of that, the complexity of the task would be horrific; it is difficult enough at the company level.

The objective of job evaluation is to clarify the relative position of jobs within an organisation, to provide a sound basis for personnel administration. The approach is impersonal. Emphasis is confined to

158

the scope and importance of the work itself. In its pure form, the contribution of an individual job incumbent, in terms of performance, potential or qualities brought to the job is eschewed. Job evaluation can produce no more than a logical, hierarchical ranking of jobs according to their content. It aims at an equitable distribution and attempts to produce an unbiased result. Whilst the analysis is intended to form the basis for pay determination, the method *per se* cannot dictate associated pay levels, for it is concerned with relationships, not with absolutes. The structure might indicate rational differences between jobs, but rarely can these be translated into corresponding pay differentials without the exercise of value judgements. Recourse must be made to market rates, to company wage or salary policies, and allowances must be made for personal factors. Job evaluation is an incomplete tool. It can only provide a skeleton framework for building a system of equitable payment.

Despite the limitations inherent in job evaluation, the contribution which it has to offer as a means for identifying, analysing and assessing the essential differences between the demands of various jobs should not be underrated. Without it, chaos and confusion, anomaly and anachronism, are likely to reign. It provides a formal, standardised basis for a pay policy. There is no one method which is superior on all counts *vis-à-vis* any other method. The techniques which have been developed have stood the test of time and are currently in common usage. They vary in their degree of sophistication, critical powers of making fine discriminations between jobs and complexity of administration. Conventional techniques are the originals and the ones which have been most commonly applied. In recent years new developments have taken place, building on their precepts and concepts. The adoption of any one particular approach will depend on the amount of time and effort an organisation is willing to expend, on the detail and accuracy required, and on the acceptability of the technique to its members and negotiating parties. Operationally, it will depend too on the type and level of job and on the occupational groupings to be evaluated. Personal preference and familiarity with a given method are also bound to exert their influence.

All of it is essentially subjective in spite of quasi-quantification. By whatever method, judgement must be exercised somewhere. Critics and cynics scorn the influence of people's minds, machinations and considered opinions. For them there is no room for human variation nor

159

unscientific deliberation. Were it not for the fact that elements of work may be intangible in terms of conventional dimensions of measurement, were it not for the fact that man's perceptual powers preclude complete rationality and objectivity, then we could live in a mathematical nicety, predestined, predictive and boring. There would be no problem. Happily, we live in reality.

Appendix 1

Factor Points Scheme (for Technical, Professional and Managerial Staff) in Operation at International Computers Ltd[1]

Job evaluation scheme:

Factor 1   Mental requirements
Factor 2   Training, experience and maturity
Factor 3   Communication requirements
Factor 4   Creative requirements
Factor 5   Discretionary responsibilities
Factor 6   Accountability
Factor 7   Personnel responsibilities

Job evaluation record form
[*contd.*]

[1] Reproduced by kind permission from *Job Evaluation—A Guide for Managers* ICL Remuneration Planning Department, 1969, revised.

1 Mental requirements

The level of general reasoning ability required to comprehend and resolve the situations normally encountered within the job.

Consider:

The nature of such situations, and whether the job-holder can apply well-understood rules and procedures or, at the other extreme, needs the ability to grasp the principles underlying complex issues.

For company salaried employees, GCE 'O' level is normally associated with 'average' reasoning ability, 'A' level with 'above average' and degree standard with a 'high' level of reasoning ability.

Level of mental ability	Points
Moderate Comprehends and resolves repetitive situations requiring the application of well-understood instructions and procedures.	10
	13
	16
Average Comprehends and resolves related situations which require the job-holder to discriminate in applying established procedures and routines.	20
	24
	28
Above average Comprehends and resolves differing and quite complex situations which require the job-holder to arrive at solutions within an area of knowledge familiar to him.	33
	38
	43
High Comprehends and resolves differing and complex situations requiring considerable breadth and/or depth of knowledge and a high degree of analytical and constructive thinking.	49
	55
	61

Very high	68
Comprehends and resolves new and highly complex situations which are identified only in terms of abstract principles and general objectives.	
	75

2 Training, experience and maturity

The level of training, the length of relevant work experience, and the degree of maturity required for successful performance of the job. Assess each factor in terms of the essential rather than the preferred standard required.

Consider:

Training

The minimum level of academic, professional, commercial or technical training normally associated with the job. Rate 'Training level' on the vertical scale.

Experience

The minimum length of post-qualifying practical experience relevant to the job in question. Rate 'Years' experience' on the horizontal scale.

Note: (a) both formal Company training and on-the-job training should be counted within experience.

(b) in the case of sandwich and professional training, experience should be counted from minimum age 21, and in any case after a minimum of 3 years' training.

Maturity

Consider the minimum age normally associated with the required degree of maturity. For example, how essential is it for the job-holder to be capable of balanced, independent thought and action; to have a realistic understanding of other people's abilities and behaviour; to be capable of taking a long as well as a short term view? Rate this factor on the 'Minimum age' scale.

Training level	Years of relevant practical experience											
	0	½	1	2	3	4	5	7	10	12	15	15+
No training specified	1	5	9	17	24	30	35	40	43	45	47	50
GCE 'O' level	10	14	18	26	33	39	44	49	52	54	56	59
ONC	12	16	20	28	35	41	46	51	54	56	58	61

163

GCE 'A' level OND	14	18	22	30	37	43	48	53	56	58	60	63
HNC HND (2 years) Intermediate or professional Final professional (1 to 2 years)	22	26	30	38	45	51	56	61	64	66	68	71
Degree HNC+endorsements HND tech. (4 year sandwich)	26	30	34	42	49	55	60	65	68	70	72	75
Honours degree (1st, 2nd) Final professional (4 to 5 years)	28	32	36	44	51	57	62	67	70	72	74	77
Degree and relevant post graduate course (PhD, MBA, MSc.) Degree and relevant professional qualifica- tion	37	41	45	53	60	66	71	76	79	81	83	86

Maturity

Minimum age	21–23	24–26	27–29	30–32	33+
Points	2	5	8	11	14

3 Communication requirements The extent to which communication skills are required for successful performance of the job. These include those skills which together constitute a facility with words; the ability to speak and write clearly and convincingly; the ability to absorb and understand information. They also include the social skills required to establish and maintain job contacts at the required level within the Company and externally.

Consider:

1. The nature of the information being received and communicated by the job-holder, i.e. oral or written, verbal or

numerical; the volume and degree of complexity. Rate this factor on the vertical scale.

2. The difficulties implicit in understanding and communicating this information, taking into account the nature and range of the job-holder's contacts, e.g. level; inside or outside the Company; with persons of similar or dissimilar background. Rate this factor on the horizontal scale within these parameters:

Minor or Moderate
The job-holder is shielded in difficult cases by the manager to whom he reports.

Appreciable or High
The job-holder is dealing on his own initiative with persons at different levels but not normally higher than the equivalent of Divisional Manager.

Major
The job-holder has contacts inside and outside the Company with senior management. The establishment and maintenance of such high level contacts is essential for the successful performance of the job.

Nature of information being received and communicated	Degree of difficulty				
	Minor	Mod.	Apprec.	High	Major
Minor Receives and communicates routine information by means of discussion or writing.	7	9	12	—	—
Moderate Receives and communicates routine and non-routine information by means of discussion or writing.	13	16	20	24	—
Appreciable Requires the ability to comprehend and communicate complex information. May be involved in difficult discussions/complex writing/routine negotiation/instruction/speaking.	19	23	28	33	38
High The volume and complexity of information received is high and requires from the job-holder a well-developed	—	31	37	43	49

capacity to comprehend and com-
municate such information. May be
involved in very difficult discussion/
negotiations/writing/instruction/
speaking.

Major	Minor	Mod.	Apprec.	High	V. High
Reserve this category for those cases where the volume and/or complexity of the information is such that the need to comprehend and communicate it dominates the nature of the job being considered.	—	—	48	54	60

4 Creative reqiurements

The extent to which a job requires the ability to initiate, devise, design or improve systems, equipment, policies, plans, procedures, etc.

Consider:

1. The nature of the innovative thinking required of the job-holder. Rate this factor on the vertical scale.
2. The scope that the job-holder has for exercising such innovative thinking. Rate this factor on the horizontal scale.

Nature of the innovative thinking required	Scope				
	Minor	Mod.	Apprec.	High	V. High
Minor The job normally requires the application of well-understood rules and procedures. Consequently the requirement for innovative thinking is not sufficiently significant to score.	—	—	—	—	—
Moderate *Technical:* Routine systems/method analysis and design. Writing programming instructions. Routine diagnosis and correction of hardware/software faults. Adaptation or revision of technical literature. *General:* Planning departmental organisation/procedures/workloads.	5	10	15	—	—

166

Appreciable
Technological: 16   21   26   31   —
Complex systems analysis and design.
Original method study and design.
Development of comparatively well-defined hardware/software concepts.
Complex diagnosis and correction of hardware/software faults.
Original writing of major technical reports or external literature.

General:
Planning implementation of new projects: planning deployment of resources.
Original writing of major non-technical reports or external literature.

High
Technological: —   32   37   42   47
Original systems design.
Design/development of only partially defined hardware/software concepts.

General:
Formulation and development of major policies/plans.

Very High
High level, original technological re-   —   —   48   54   60
search.

---

5 Discretionary responsibilities   The extent of responsibility for making decisions and taking action in relation to activities affecting the business of the Company, or making recommendations which are invariably implemented by virtue of their specialist nature, or positively influence the decisions made by others.

Consider:

1. The significance of the decisions or recommendations in relation to the activity concerned, and the importance of that activity relative to others in the Company.

2. The extent to which responsibility may be exercised as determined by the parameters of the job. Assess whether, for example, there is:

167

— limited scope to act according to own judgement; few decisions implemented without reference to immediate manager;

— some scope to act according to own judgement; decisions often implemented without reference to immediate manager;

— wide scope to act according to own judgement; few decisions need to be referred to immediate manager.

Significance of decisions and recommendations	Points
Minor	
Decisions, within set procedures which affect only the means by which an objective is achieved, and not the objective itself.	6
Recommendations normally routine in nature, which influence the achievement of individual group objectives, and which affect only a very limited area of the Company's business.	12
	18
Moderate	
Decisions, normally routine in nature and following existing precedent, which concern the achievement of subsidiary group objectives, and affect only a very limited area of the Company's business.	24
	30
Recommendations of a technical or specialised nature, which influence the work of a department, and which affect a specific area of the Company's business.	36
Appreciable	
Decisions, often non-routine in nature, which concern the achievement of a department's function and which affect a specific area of the Company's business.	42
	50
Recommendations of a very technical or specialised nature, which influence the work of an important function, and which affect an important area of the Company's business.	58

High

Decisions, invariably on important matters, which concern the organisation and direction of an important function, and which affect a significant area of the Company's business.	66
	74
Recommendations of a highly technical or specialised nature, which influence the work of a major function and which affect a considerable area of the Company's business.	82

Major

Decisions, invariably on highly important matters, which concern the formulation and implementation of Company policy, and which affect the total business of the Company.	90
	100

6 Accountability   The influence on the Company's business of any act or omission which may occur on the job, and the likelihood of this occurring. Consider:

1. The possible effect of failure, as revealed by the range and type of activities for which the job-holder can be called to account, e.g. Company assets, customer and employee relations, projects and expenditure.
2. The possibility of failure occurring, as revealed by the degree to which checks operate, the time-span before they operate, and the difficulty of remedying mistakes.

Effect of failure	Points
Minor	
Some effect on unit within which job is performed. Minimal effect on other activities. No effect on Company business.	3
	6
	9

169

Moderate

Moderate effect on the output of a work group.   12
Some effect on other activities.
Minimal effect on Company business.

15

18

Appreciable

Appreciable effect on the output of work group.   21
Moderate effect on other activities which could
result in failure to meet functional time-scales/stan-

---

dards/output levels.
Limited effect on total Company business.   25

29

High

Considerable effect on an important function, and   33
the activities resulting from this function.
Considerable effect on other important functions,

---

which could result in failure to meet significant
time-scales/standard/output levels. Some effect on   37
total Company business.

41

Major

Very considerable effect on a major function, and   45
the activities resulting from this function.
Very considerable effect on other major functions,

---

which could result in failure to meet major time-
scales/standard/output levels. Significant effect on   50
total Company business, where failure could result
in major loss of business or unnecessarily high

---

expenditure.

---

7 Personnel responsibilities The importance of the responsibility for selection, general control, welfare, training, safety, discipline and review of performance and salary of personnel under the control of the job-holder.

Consider:

1. The number of personnel under the control of the job-holder. Note: In cases of temporary control (e.g. during instruction), the average number involved at any one time should be halved for the purpose of this assessment.

2. The difficulties implicit in this responsibility, taking into account the type and dispersal of personnel controlled, and the degree to which a complete responsibility for all aspects of personnel management, must be exercised. Also consider whether the job-holder must directly control personnel under him, or is able to delegate much of this responsibility to subordinates.

Number of staff controlled	Degree of difficulty				
	Minor	Mod.	Apprec.	High	V. High
1 to 10	2	5	9	13	—
10 to 50	6	10	14	18	22
50 to 100	—	17	21	25	29
100 to 500	—	—	28	32	36
500+	—	—	37	41	45

International Computers Group

Technical professional and managerial staff

Job evaluation record

	Organisation	Division	Department		Date
Group					
Committee					
Job code					
Job title					
Region/CSS/S(Sup)					
Minimum/Lower Bar					
Control					
Upper Bar/Maximum					
Factor points					
1 Mental requirements					
2 Training and experience					
Maturity					
3 Communication requirements					
4 Creative requirements					
6 Discretionary responsibilities					
6 Accountability					
7 Personnel responsibilities					
Total					
Specification					
Minimum academic/training level					
Minimum years' experience					
Number of staff controlled					
Review code					

FORM 4/250(5.72)

Appendix II

Factor Points Rating Scheme
Developed by Associated Industrial Consultants/Inbucon Ltd
for the Senior Salary Structure of the Post Office.[1]

Job evaluation scheme:

Factor 1 Background
Factor 2 Decisions
Factor 3 Judgement
Factor 4 Leadership
Factor 5 Contacts

JOB EVALUATION
SUMMARY OF FACTORS

Factor	Maximum Points
1 Background	17
2 Decisions	25
3 Judgement	40
4 Leadership	9
5 Contacts	9
Maximum Points	100

[1] Reproduced by kind permission of AIC and the Post Office.

JOB EVALUATION
FACTOR 1

Background—The knowledge and experience which are needed to perform the job successfully.

Concentrate on:

  a **Knowledge:** Vocational training; technical or specialised knowledge needed.

  b **Experience:** Extent and diversity required.

a **Knowledge**		b **Experience**	
Degree	**Description**	**Degree**	**Description**
I	Basic	I	Sufficient to undertake a middle management post
II	Intermediate	II	Equivalent to that required for the immediate control of management posts
III	Good	III	Longer and more varied; fitting for a wide range of management posts
IV	Higher	IV	Wide variety; usually both inside and outside HQ, or suitably specialised for senior technical/specialist posts
V	Expert	V	Extensive: varied and at high level

Notes: 1. Any Degree of Knowledge can be combined with any Degree of Experience.

        2. The wording of the degree description is intended as a guide. Consider the job as a whole and place it in the degree which seems the nearest fit.

JOB EVALUATION
FACTOR 2

Decisions—The decisions taken on the job-holder's own authority.

Concentrate on decisions not recommendations: that is, on the job-holder's power to commit the use of Post Office resources—money, staff, facilities—and his accountability for:

Making the commitment.
The value obtained from it.
The consequences of the decisions.

Degree	Description
I	Decisions only within well-defined rules or precedents.
II	More difficult decisions, still within rules and precedents, and concerned with a minor part of the Post Office's resources.
III	Decisions with distinction permitted within rules and precedents. Modest Post Office resources likely to be involved.
IV	Wide discretion within defined limits. Post Office resources of some importance involved.
V	Decisions involving important Post Office resources.
VI	Decisions involving Post Office resources of considerable importance.
VII	Decisions which commit a significant part of total Post Office resources and have far-reaching consequences.
VIII	Decisions which commit fundamental Post Office resources and have fundamental consequences for the future of the business.

Note: The wording of the degree description is intended as a guide. Consider the job as a whole and place it in the degree which seems the nearest fit.

JOB EVALUATION
FACTOR 3

Judgement—The process of selecting or recommending a course of action by analysis and appraisal of alternatives.
Concentrate on:

a	**Complexity and Importance:**	The complexity of analysis required. The versatility required in handling various problems. The importance to the Post Office of correct judgement.
b	**Intangibility:**	The difficulty of determining with certainty the full effects of alternative courses.

a Complexity and Importance

Complexity:	**Importance:**
The complexity of analysis required.	The importance to the Post Office of correct judgement.
The versatility required in handling various problems.	

Degree	Description	Degree	Description
I	Generally straightforward. problems, clearly defined, and needing little versatility.	A	Correct judgement of minor importance to the Post Office.
		B	Correct judgement of limited importance to the Post Office.
II	Varied and sometimes complicated problems requiring a moderate degree of versatility.	B	Correct judgement of limited importance to the Post Office.
		C	Correct judgement of moderate importance to the Post Office.
III	Diverse and more complicated problems involving considerable versatility, and which are capable of a number of solutions.	C	Correct judgement of moderate importance to the Post Office.
		D	Correct judgment of considerable importance to the Post Office.
IV	Complex problems involving a number of aspects of the business.	D	Correct judgement of considerable importance to the Office.
		E	Correct judgement of major importance to the Post Office.
V	Highly complex problems covering a wide range of the activities of the business.	E	Correct judgement of major importance to the Post Office.
		F	Correct judgement of fundamental importance to the Post Office.

176

b **Intangibility**

The difficulty of determining with certainty the full effect of alternative courses.

Degree	Description
I	Work in well-trodden fields in which judgement is greatly helped by precedent and experience.
II	Work in which judgement is generally helped by precedent and experience, but in which judgement in new fields is sometimes necessary.
III	Work where the problems are often unpredecented and the effect of different recommendations is difficult to assess.
IV	Work generally of a pioneering nature where it is impossible to predict closely the effect of alternative courses.

Notes: 1. Any Degree of Complexity can be combined with either Degree of Importance listed with it. The resulting Degree can then be combined with any Degree of Intangibility.
2. The wording of the degree description is intended as a guide. Consider the job as a whole and place it in the degree which seems the nearest fit.

JOB EVALUATION

FACTOR 4

Leadership—Persuading subordinates to adopt a particular course of action and getting the best out of them.

Concentrate on:

The size of the group led and the character of their work.
The nature of the opposition likely to be encountered.
The extent to which groups with varying interests have to be welded and led.
(Consider subordinate staff only)

Degree	Description
I	Leadership not a significant part of the job.
II	Leadership of a small group involving some difficulty for the leader or of a large group but with few problems.
III	Leadership of a number of different specialists giving rise to difficulties or a large or scattered group involving leadership problems.
IV	Leadership of an important body of staff responsible for a significant part of the activities of the business.
V	Leadership requirement of the highest importance because of difficult problems, large and scattered numbers, or widely varied specialisms.

Note: The wording of the degree description is intended as a guide. Consider the job as a whole and place it in the degree which seems the nearest fit.

177

JOB EVALUATION
FACTOR 5

Contacts—Dealing with or influencing people other than subordinates, e.g. within the Post Office, members of the public, suppliers, government department, staff associations.

Concentrate on:

> The level of the contacts.
> The range or diversity of contacts.
> The importance to the Post Office of proper handling of the contacts.

Degree	Description
I	Few or limited contacts.
II	Some liaison with others necessary for the successful undertaking of the job.
III	Regular contacts necessary inside and/or outside the Post Office but not generally constituting a major aspect of the work.
IV	Dealing with and influencing others frequently necessary and of considerable importance to the business.
V	The successful influencing of others at high level a major aspect of the work and of fundamental importance to the business.

Note: The wording of the degree description is intended as a guide. Consider the job as a whole and place it in the degree which seems the nearest fit.

Appendix III

An Extract from the TUC 20-Factor Plan [1]

Job evaluation scheme:

Factor 1	Education	(General requirements)
Factor 2	Training	(General requirements)
Factor 3	Previous experience	(General requirements)
Factor 4	Initiation period	(General requirements)
Factor 5	Variety of work	(General requirements)
Factor 6	Dexterity	(General requirements)
Factor 7	Observation	(General requirements)
Factor 8	Executive ability	(Special requirements)
Factor 9	Analytical ability	(Special requirements)
Factor 10	Development	(Special requirements)
Factor 11	Responsibility for labour	(Responsibilities)
Factor 12	Responsibility for materials	(Responsibilities)
Factor 13	Responsibility for equipment	(Responsibilities)
Factor 14	Responsibility for clerical work	(Responsibilities)
Factor 15	Responsibility for contacts	(Responsibilities)
Factor 16	Monotony	(Physical requirements)
Factor 17	Abnormal positions	(Physical requirements)
Factor 18	Abnormally heavy work	(Physical requirements)
Factor 19	Disagreeable conditions	(Physical requirements)
Factor 20	Hazards of injury or accident	(Physical requirements)

[contd.]

[1] Reproduced by kind permission from *Job Evaluation and Merit Rating* (Trades Union Congress, 1969, 2nd edn.).

GENERAL REQUIREMENTS

Points range

1 *Education*   0–20

2 *Training*
(a) Technical or Commercial Qualifications   0–45
(b) Apprenticeship—4 points per year   0–20

3 *Previous experience*
Consider the minimum age at which the average person could undertake this job, $1\frac{1}{2}$ points for every year over 15 in the case of elementary or 16 in the case of secondary education (exclude apprenticeship years if any).   0–40

4 *Initiation Period*
The period required by an experienced person to undertake the job:
Low—1 week to 1 month   0–4
Medium—1 month to 6 months   5–7
High—7 months to 12 months   8–10

5 *Variety of Work*
Consider whether the complexity of the work or process requires the mastery of an unusual number of details.
Low   0–5
Medium   6–10
High   11–15

6 *Dexterity*
Consider whether unusual quickness or deftness is required to do the work successfully, or whether the close co-ordination of eyes and muscles is demanded.
Low   0–3
Medium   4–7
High   8–10

7 *Observation*
This denotes alertness required to details of the product, equipment, processes or buildings.
Low   0–5
Medium   6–10
High   11–20

SPECIAL REQUIREMENTS

8 *Executive Ability*
Consider the job requirements in so far as tact, the ability to secure co-operation of others and the selection and development of subordinates are concerned.
Low   0–20
Medium   21–30
High   31–40
Higher   41–80

Points range

9 *Analytical Ability*
    This denotes the ability to obtain and interpret data relevant to the
    work in hand and to plan suitable action.
Low	0–10
Medium	11–20
High	21–30
Higher	31–40

10 *Development*
    Consider the extent to which the job demands the origination of
    new schemes or processes.
Low	0–10
Medium	11–30
High	31–40

The other 10 factors in this scheme include responsibilities (for labour, material, equipment, clerical work and contacts) and physical requirements (monotony, abnormal positions, abnormally heavy work, disagreeable conditions, possible severity of injury from any accident).

Appendix IV

Local Government Staff (Greater London) Job Evaluation Scheme[1]

Job evaluation scheme:

- Factor 1   Experience
- Factor 2   Education
- Factor 3   Supervisory
- Factor 4   Decisions made
- Factor 5   Work complexity
- Factor 6   Records and reports
- Factor 7   Contacts
- Factor 8   Supervision received
- Factor 9   Assets and materials

Local Government Staff (Greater London) Job Evaluation Scheme

Factor	No. of Subfactors	Maximum No. of Points
Experience	13	160
Education	11	120
Supervisory	9	80
Decisions made	9	100
Work complexity	7	80
Records and reports	7	80
Contacts	9	80
Supervision received	9	50
Assets and materials	9	50

[1] Reproduced from: THOMSON, T. G. (1968) Job Evaluation for Non-Manual Workers: Local Government Staff in Greater London.
International Labour Review, 98 (Dec.), 511-524.

Bibliography

ADAMS, J. S. (1963), 'Towards an Understanding of Inequity', *Journal of Abnormal and Social Psychology*, **67**, 422–36.

ADAMS, J. S. (1965), 'Injustice to Social Change' in Berkowitz, L. (ed.) (1965), *Advances in Experimental Social Psychology*, Vol. **2**, 267–99 (London: Academic Press).

ATKINSON, J. W. (ed.) (1958), *Motives in Fantasy, Action, and Society* (London: Van Nostrand).

BARTH, C. G. (1921), 'Stop Watch Time Studies', *Bulletin of the Taylor Society*, **6**, 108–11.

BELCHER, D. W. (1963), *Wage and Salary Administration* (New York: Prentice Hall).

BENDIX, R. (1956), *Work and Authority in Industry* (New York: Wiley).

BENGE, E. J., BURK, S. L. H., and HAY, E. N. (1941), *Manual of Job Evaluation* (New York: Harper & Row).

BLOCH, W. (1951), 'Arbeitsbewertung in der Schweiz', *Industrielle Organisation*, **27**, 10.

BRITISH INSTITUTE OF MANAGEMENT (1970), *Job Evaluation* (London: Management Publications Ltd).

BRITISH STANDARDS INSTITUTION (1969), *Glossary of Terms Used in Work Study*, BS 3138, A3001 (London: British Standards Institution).

BROWN, W. (1973), *The Earnings Conflict* (London: Heinemann).

CAREY, A. (1967), 'The Hawthorne Studies: A Radical Criticism', *American Sociological Review*, **32**, 3. Reprinted in *Bobbs-Merrill Reprint Series in the Social Sciences* (1967), 401–6.

CELTINGER, M. P. (1964), 'Nationwide Job Evaluation in the Netherlands', *Industrial Relations*, October **64**, 45–49.

CENTRAL ORGANISATION OF SALARIED EMPLOYEES, SWEDEN (1966), *Job Classification and Collective Bargaining*, TCO International Seminar, papers and summary of discussions (Stockholm: TCO).

CHESLER, D. J. (1948), 'Reliability and Comparability of Different Job Evaluation Systems', *Journal of Applied Psychology*, **32**, 622–8.

CHRISTAL, R. E., MADDEN, J. M. and HARDING, F. D. (1960), *Reliability of Job Evaluation Ratings as a Function of Number of Raters and Length of Job Descriptions Used* (Lackland Air Force Base, Texas: Personnel Laboratory, Wright Air Development Division, WADD-TN-60-257).

CLEGG, H. (1971), *How to Run an Incomes Policy* (London: Heinemann).

CLIFF, T. (1970), *The Employer's Offensive—Productivity Deals and How to Fight Them* (London: Pluto Press).

DANIEL, W. W. (1970), *Beyond the Wage-Work Bargain* (London: Political and Economic Planning).

DOLLARD, J. and MILLER, N. E. (1950), *Personality and Psychotherapy* (New York: McGraw Hill).

DUNNETTE, M. D. (1965), *Factor Structures of Unusually Satisfying and Unusually Dissatisfying Job Situations for Six Occupational Groups* (Chicago: Midwestern Psychological Association).

183

ELLIOTT, A. G. P. (1960), *Staff Grading* (London: British Institute of Management).

EVANS, J. S. (1970), 'Time-Span: The Neglected Tool', *Personnel Management*, **2**, 2, 28–39.

FESTINGER, L. (1957), *A Theory of Cognitive Dissonance* (Stanford University Press).

FLANAGAN, J. C. (1954), 'The Critical Incident Technique', *Psychological Bulletin*, **51**, 327–58.

FOX, A. (1966), *Industrial Sociology and Industrial Relations*, Research Paper 3, Royal Commission on Trade Unions and Employers Associations (London: HMSO).

FULTON REPORT: THE CIVIL SERVICE (1968), Cmnd 3638 (London: HMSO).

GEORGOPOULOS, B. S., MAHONEY, G. M., and JONES, N. W. (1957), 'Path-Goal Approach to Productivity, *Journal of Applied Psychology*, **41**, 345–53.

GILBERT, M. H. (1970), 'The Asset Value of the Human Organisation', *Management Accounting*, July 1970 (New York: National Association of Accountants).

GILES, W. J. and ROBINSON, D. F. (1972), *Human Asset Accounting* (London: Institute of Personnel Management and Institute of Cost and Works Accountants).

GOLDENBERG, S. J. (1968), 'Significant Difference: A Method of Job Evaluation', *The Canadian Personnel and Industrial Relations Journal*, **15**, 3, 19–21.

GOLDSTEIN, K. (1939), *The Organism: a Holistic Approach to Biology Derived from Pathological Data in Man* (New York: American Book Company).

GOLDTHORPE, J. H., LOCKWOOD, D., BECHHOFFER, F., PLATT, J. (1968), *The Affluent Worker: Industrial Attitudes and Behaviour* (Cambridge University Press).

GOMBERG, W. (1951), 'A Trade Unionist Looks at Job Evaluation', *Journal of Applied Psychology*, **35**, 1–7.

GOODMAN, P. S. (1967), 'An Empirical Examination of Elliot Jaques's Concept of Timespan', *Human Relations*, **20**, 2, 155–70.

HAY, E. N. and PURVES, D. (1951), 'A New Method of Job Evaluation—The Guide Chart Profile Method', *Personnel*, **28**, 162–70.

HAZEWINKEL, A. (1969), 'Job Evaluation as a Measuring Procedure', *Proceedings. International Conference on Job Evaluation, Amsterdam*, European Work Study Federation and European Association for Personnel Management (The Hague: Nederlands Instituut voor Efficiency).

HEKIMIAN, J. S. and JONES, C. H. (1967), 'Put People on Your Balance Sheet', *Harvard Business Review*, January/February 1967, 105–13.

HENLEY, J. S. (1972), 'Salary Administration', *Personnel Management*, **4**, 4, 28–30.

HERZBERG F., MAUSNER, B., and SNYDERMAN, B. (1959), *The Motivation to Work* (New York: Wiley).

HERZBERG, F. (1968), *Work and the Nature of Man* (London: Staples Press).

HESSE, H. (1927), *Steppenwolf* (Frankfurt: S. Fischer Verlag A.G.; Harmondsworth: Penguin Books (1965)).

HOMANS, G. C. (1951), *The Human Group* (London: Routlege & Kegan Paul).

HOMANS, G. C. (1961), *Social Behaviour: Its Elementary Forms* (London: Routledge & Kegan Paul).

HOUSE, R. J. and WIGDOR, L. A. (1967), 'Herzberg's Dual-factor Theory of Job Satisfaction and Motivation: A Review of the Evidence and a Criticism, *Personnel Psychology*, **50**, 280–5.

HULIN, C. L., and BLOOD, M. R. (1968), 'Job Enlargement, Individual Differences and Worker Responses', *Psychological Bulletin*, **69**, 1, 41–55.

HULL, C. L. (1931), 'Goal Attraction and Directing Ideas Conceived as Habit Phenomena, *Psychological Review*, **38**, 487–506.

HULL, C. L. (1943), *Principles of Behaviour* (New York: Appleton-Century Crofts).

INSTITUTE OF OFFICE MANAGEMENT (1964), *Clerical Job Grading Schedule* (London).

INTERNATIONAL ASSOCIATION OF MACHINISTS (1954), *What's Wrong with Job Evaluation* (Washington).

INTERNATIONAL COMPUTERS LIMITED (1969, Revised), *Job Evaluation (Technical, Professional, Managerial)—A Guide for Managers* (London: ICL Remuneration Planning Department).

JAQUES, E. (1961), *Equitable Payment* (London: Heinemann).

JAQUES, E. (1964), *Time-Span Handbook* (London: Heinemann).

JAQUES, E. (1967), *Equitable Payment: A General Theory of Work, Differential Payment and Individual Progress* (Harmondsworth: Penguin Books, 'Pelican Library of Business Management').

JAQUES, E. (1967), *Progression Handbook* (London: Heinemann).

JAQUES, E. (1969), 'Fair Pay: How to Achieve It', *New Society*, November 1969.

JAQUES, E. (1970), *Work, Creativity and Social Justice* (London: Heinemann).

KORDASZEWSKI, J. (1969), 'A Polish Contribution to Job Evaluation for Non-Manual Workers', *International Labour Review*, August 1969, 140–57.

KRESS, A. L. (1939), 'How to Rate Jobs and Men', *Factory Management*, **97**, 60–5.

LANER, S. and CAPLAN, S. (1969), *Earnings Progression Data Sheets Expressed in US Dollars* (HFT Report 69-2/ONR Technical Report, University of California).

LANHAM, E. (1955), *Job Evaluation* (New York: McGraw Hill).

LAWLER, E. E. and PORTER, L. W. (1967), 'Antecedent Attitudes of Effective Managerial Performance'. *Organisational Behavior and Human Performance*, **2**, 122–42.

LAWLER, E. E. and PORTER, L. W. (1967). 'The Effect of Performance on Job Satisfaction', *Industrial Relations*, **7**, 20–8.

LAWLER, E. E. (1971), *Pay and Organisational Effectiveness: A Psychological View* (New York: McGraw Hill).

LAWSHE, C. H. and SATTER, G. A. (1944), 'Studies in Job Evaluation: I. Factor Analysis of Point Ratings for Hourly Paid Jobs in Three Industrial Plants, *Journal of Applied Psychology*, **28**, 189–98.

LAWSHE, C. H. (1945), 'Studies in Job Evaluation: II. The Adequacy of Abbreviated Point Ratings for Hourly Paid Jobs in Three Industrial Plants, *Journal of Applied Psychology*, **29**, 177–84.

LAWSHE, C. H. and MALESKI, A. A. (1946), 'Studies in Job Evaluation: III An analysis of Point Ratings for Salary Paid Jobs in an Industrial Plant'. *Journal of Applied Psychology*, **30**, 117–28.

LEWIN, K. (1935), *A Dynamic Theory of Personality* (Maidenhead: McGraw Hill).

LEWIN, K. (1936), *Principles of Topological Psychology* (New York: McGraw Hill).

LEWIN, K. (1938), *The Conceptual Representation and the Measurement of Psychological Forces* (Durham NC: Duke University Press).

LIKERT, R. (1967), *The Human Organisation: Its Management and Value*, (Maidenhead: McGraw Hill).

LIPPITT, G. L. (1969), *Organisational Review* (New York: Appleton Century Crofts).

LIVERNASH, E. R. (1954), 'Wage Administration and Production Standards', in

Kornhauser, A., Dubin, R., and Ross, A. M. (eds), *Industrial Conflict* (Maidenhead: McGraw Hill).

LOTT, M. R. (1926), *Wage Scales and Job Evaluation* (New York: Ronald Press).

LUPTON, T. and GOWLER, D. (1969), *Selecting a Wage Payment System*, Federation Research Paper III (London: Engineering Employers' Federation).

LYONS, T. P. (1971), *The Personnel Function in a Changing Environment* (London: Pitman).

MCBEATH, G. (1969), *Management Remuneration Policy* (London: Business Books).

MCDOUGALL, C. (1973), 'How Well Do You Reward Your Managers', *Personnel Management*, 5, 3, 38–43.

MCGREGOR, D. (1960), *The Human Side of Enterprise* (Maidenhead: McGraw Hill).

MAHLER, W. R. (1950), 'Let's Get More Scientific in Rating Employees, in Dooher, M. J. and Marquis, V. (eds), *Rating Employee and Supervisory Performance* (New York: American Management Association).

MASLOW, A. H. (1943), 'A Theory of Human Motivation', *Psychological Review*, 50, 370–96.

MASLOW, A. H. (1954), *Motivation and Personality* (New York (London 1970): Harper & Row).

MORGAN, V. (1973), 'Civil Service Pay: Role of the Pay Research Unit', *Personnel Management*, 5, 4, 26–8.

MYERS, M. S. (1964), 'Who Are Your Motivated Workers?' *Harvard Business Review*, 42 (i) 73–88.

NATIONAL BOARD FOR PRICES AND INCOMES (1968), *Job Evaluation*, Report No. 83 (London: HMSO).

NATIONAL BOARD FOR PRICES AND INCOMES (1968), *Salary Structures*, Report No. 132 (London: HMSO).

NATIONAL WHITLEY COUNCIL (1972), *The Shape of the Post-Fulton Civil Service* (London: HMSO).

OPSAHL, R. L. and DUNNETTE, M. D. (1966), 'The Role of Financial Compensation in Industrial Motivation', *Psychological Bulletin*, 66, 94–118.

OTIS, J. L. and LEUKART, R. H. (1954, 2nd edn), *Job Evaluation* (Englewood Cliffs, NJ: Prentice Hall).

PATERSON, T. T. (1969), 'The Decision Band Method', *Proceedings. International Conference on Job Evaluation, Amsterdam*, European Work Study Federation and European Association for Personnel Management (The Hague: Nederlands Instituut voor Efficiency).

PATERSON, T. T. and HUSBAND, T. M. (1970), 'Decision-Making Responsibility: Yardstick for Job Evaluation', *Compensation Review*, second quarter (spring), 21–31.

PATERSON, T. T. (1972), *Job Evaluation. Vol. 1. A New Method* (London: Business Books).

PATERSON, T. T. (1972), *Job Evaluation. Vol. 2. A Manual for the Paterson Method* (London: Business Books).

PATERSON, T. T. (1972), 'Can jobs be systematically graded?', *The Times*, 6 March 1972.

PATON, W. A. (1932), *The Accountants' Handbook* (New York: Ronald Press Company).

PATTON, J. A., LITTLEFIELD, C. L., SELF, S. A. (1964, 3rd edn), *Job Evaluation—Text and Cases* (Homewood, Il: Richard D. Irwin, Inc.).

PORTER, L. W. (1961), 'A Study of Perceived Need Satisfaction in Bottom and Middle Management Jobs, *Journal of Applied Psychology*, **45**, 1–10.

PORTER, L. W. (1962), 'Job Attitudes in Management: I Perceived Deficiencies in Need Fulfilment as a Function of Job Level,' *Journal of Applied Psychology*, **46**, 375–84.

PORTER, L. W. (1963), 'Job Attitudes in Management: II Perceived Importance of Needs as a Function of Job Level,' *Journal of Applied Psychology*, **47**, 141–48.

PORTER, L. W. (1964), *Organisational Patterns of Managerial Job Attitudes* (New York: American Foundation for Management Research).

RANDALL, G. A., PACKARD, P. M. A., SHAW, R. L., SLATER, A. J. (1972), *Staff Appraisal* (London: Institute of Personnel Management).

RICHARDSON, R. (1971), *Fair Pay and Work* (London: Heinemann).

ROETHLISBERGER, F. J. and DICKSON, W. J. (1939), *Management and the Worker* (*Harvard University Press*).

ROFF, H. E. and WATSON, T. E. (1961), *Job Analysis* (London: Institute of Personnel Management).

SALES, W. H. and DAVIES, J. L. (1957), 'Introducing a New Wage Structure into Coalmining,' *Bulletin of the Oxford University Institute of Statistics*, August 1957, 201–24.

SATTER, G. A. (1949), 'Method of Paired Comparisons and a Specification scoring Key in the Evaluation of Jobs, *Journal of Applied Psychology*, **33**, 212–21.

SCHWARZ, M. M., JENUSAITIS, E. and STARK, H. (1963), 'Motivational Factors among Supervisors in the Utility Industry', *Personnel Psychology*, **16**, 45–53.

STEWART, R. (1967), *Managers and Their Jobs* (London: Macmillan).

STIEBER, J. (1959), *The Steel Industry Wage Structure: A Study of the Joint Union-Management Job Evaluation Program in the Basic Steel Industry* (Harvard University Press, 'Wertheim Publications in Industrial Relations').

SYKES, A. J. M. (1965), 'Economic Interest and the Hawthorne Researches', *Human Relations*, **18**, 253–68.

TAFT, R. (1962), 'The Ability to Judge People', in Whistler, T. L. and Harper, S. F., *Performance Appraisal* (London: Holt, Rinehart & Winston).

TAYLOR, F. W. (1911), *Principles of Scientific Management* (New York: Harper & Row).

THOMASON, G. T. (1968), *Personnel Manager's Guide to Job Evaluation* (London: Institute of Personnel Management).

THOMSON, T. G. (1968), 'Job Evaluation for Non-Manual Workers: Local Government Staff in Greater London', *International Labour Review*, December 1968, 511–24.

THORNDIKE, E. L. (1920), 'A Constant Error in Psychological Ratings', *Journal of Applied Psychology*, **4**, 25–9.

TOLMAN, E. C. (1932), *Purposive Behaviour in Animals and Men* (New York: Appleton-Century Crofts).

TRADES UNION CONGRESS (1969, 2nd edn), *Job Evaluation and Merit Rating* (London).

UHRBROCK, R. S. (1935), *A Psychologist Looks at Wage Incentive Methods* (New York: American Management Association, 'Institute of Management Series', No. 15).

VITELES, M. S. (1932), *Industrial Psychology* (New York: Norton).

VITELES, M. S. (1954), *Motivation and Morale in Industry* (London: Staples Press).

VROOM, V. (1964), *Work and Motivation* (Chichester: Wiley).

VROOM, V. (1968), 'Industrial Social Psychology', in Lindzey, G. and Aronson, E. (eds), *The Handbook of Social Psychology*, Vol. 5, 2nd edn (London: Addison-Wesley Publishing Company).

WOOTTON, B. (1955), *The Social Foundations of Wage Policy* (London: Allen & Unwin).

ZERGA, J. E. (1943), 'Job Analysis, a Résumé and Bibliography', *Journal of Applied Psychology* 27, 249–67.

ZOETEWEIJ, B. (1955), 'National Wage Policy: The Experience of the Netherlands', *International Labour Review*, 70, 2.

Index